LIFESAVING POEMS

LIFESAVING POEMS

edited by

ANTHONY WILSON

BLOODAXE BOOKS

ISBN: 978 1 78037 157 3

First published 2015 by
Bloodaxe Books Ltd,
Eastburn,
South Park,
Hexham,
Northumberland NE46 1BS.

www.bloodaxebooks.com
For further information about Bloodaxe titles
please visit our website or write to
the above address for a catalogue.

Printed in Great Britain by Bell & Bain Limited, Glasgow, Scotland, on acid-free paper sourced from mills with FSC chain of custody certification.

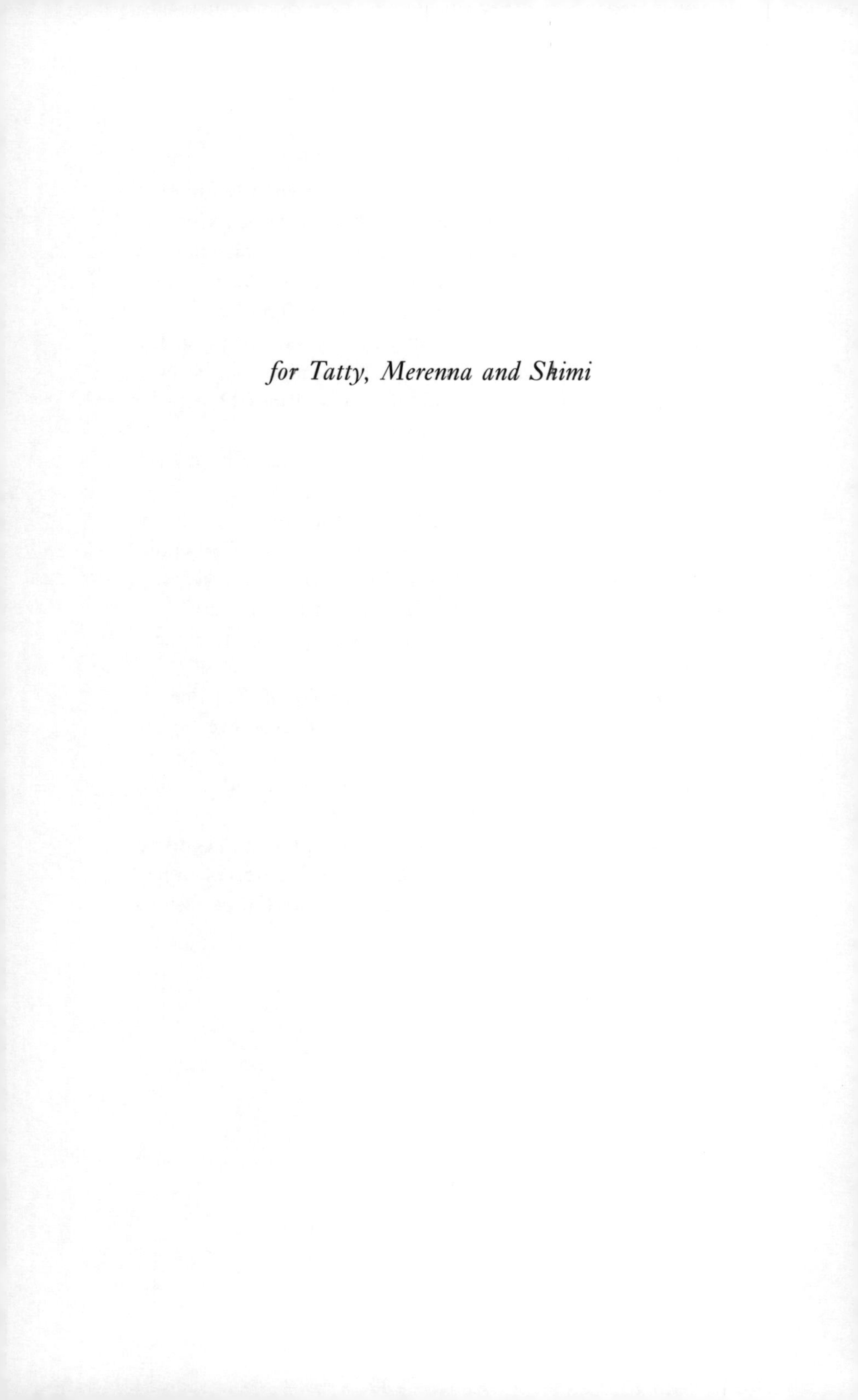

for Tatty, Merenna and Shimi

ACKNOWLEDGEMENTS

The pieces gathered here first appeared, in slightly different form, at www.anthonywilsonpoetry.com. Fragments of the pieces on Raymond Carver, Siân Hughes, Sharon Olds, Jo Shapcott and Cliff Yates first appeared in *The North*. Fragments of the Introduction and the piece on John Logan first appeared in 'The Power of Poetry', a keynote speech at the annual conference of the National Association of Teaching English, June 2014. I am indebted to Malcolm Doney for his permission to quote from his blog.

For her help with the preparation of this manuscript I am indebted to Anna Clarke.

I am deeply grateful to the following for their friendship, support and conversation: Andy Brown, Peter Carpenter, Mandy Coe, Rose Cook, Maura Dooley, Sue Dymoke, Ann Gray, Naomi Jaffa, Michael Laskey, Lawrence Sail, Ann Sansom, Peter Sansom, Christopher Southgate, Jean Sprackland and Cliff Yates.

I am indebted to the inspirational teaching of Tim Borton, Perdita Hooper and John Vickery. Your influence lives in me every day.

This book would not exist without the friendship and influence of Duncan Kramer.

Acknowledgements to the copyright sources of poems in this anthology are given after each poem. Where not otherwise specified, permission has been given by the publishers cited.

CONTENTS

'Questions unanswered'

'Heavens, I recognise the place, I know it!'

'We're still here'

C'mon people, this poetry ain't gonna appreciate itself

BART SIMPSON

INTRODUCTION

My early poetic experiences were not "poetic" at all. They were, in the main, not connected to books, and were largely to do with what I now recognise as oral forms of literature. These included riddles and puns, lullabies sung by my grandmother, playground and nursery rhymes, and hymns sung in church. Up to the age of thirteen, I cannot remember being asked to read poetry at school, except as a way of practising "correct pronunciation". My early experiences of what Auden calls 'memorable speech', were largely spontaneous, therefore, nearly always spoken, and frequently contained a mixture of simple rhyme, rhythm and humour.

Mostly this comprised what Michael Rosen calls 'stuff': adverts ('Opal Fruits, made to make your mouth water!'); my father's *Max Boyce Live* and Simon and Garfunkel tapes in the car; and playground rhymes ('Georgie Best / Superstar /He looks like a woman / And he wears a bra'). I loved the recitation of the football scores each Saturday evening on *Grandstand*, their gorgeous unpredictive text simultaneously an exotic litany (with phrases like 'Queen of the South' and 'Inverness Caledonian Thistle') and prayer. They were as important to me as the shipping forecast was to Seamus Heaney, perfectly structured and endlessly variable, joy and disappointment hiding in their cadences and inflexions: 'Chelsea 2, Arsenal 1'. But more often, as this was the 70s, disappointment.

My 'linguistic hardcore' (Heaney) did not find a counterpart in the literature of books until – aged 13 – I encountered the teaching of Tim Borton, who showed us John Logan's 'The Picnic'. It is not underestimating the case to say it changed me forever. Because of it, I still think of reading poems as like falling in love.

Lifesaving Poems began life as notebook, then a blog. Its impulse came from a remark made by Seamus Heaney in an interview. He wondered out loud if it were possible to quantify the number of poems that can affect one across a lifetime. Was it ten, he said, twenty, fifty, a hundred, or more?

As a way of trying to answer his question I began copying out poems into a plain Moleskine notebook, one at a time, in inky longhand, when the mood took me. My criteria were extremely basic.

Was the poem one I could recall having an experience with the moment I first read it? Could I live without it? To make things interesting, I allowed myself no more than one poem per poet. I quickly realised it was an acutely subjective and unscientific exercise. Frequently, the poem that was copied into my book was not especially famous, certainly not representative or even the "best" of that poet's work.

Lifesaving Poems is, therefore, not designed to be a perfect list of the great and the good. It is a group of poems I happen to feel passionate about, according to my tastes. As Billy Collins says somewhere: 'Good poems are poems that I like'.

Readers of my blog and my memoir *Love for Now* will also know that, quite apart from the physical effort of copying the poems, the notebook and subsequent blog mean much more to me. This is because, during my treatment for cancer in 2006 I felt for the first time in my life that poetry was leaving me. By that I mean not just the desire (or ability, or concentration) to write poems, but the notion of reading and spending time with poems at all.

Lifesaving Poems is therefore an attempt to say thank you, ultimately to poetry for not deserting me but also to the poets who wrote the poems, and the people – teachers, friends, colleagues, poets, anthologists – who have influenced my reading, and therefore my life, so richly.

A word about Bart Simpson. The epigraph at the head of this anthology comes from an early episode of *The Simpsons*. In an effort to control the behaviour of their errant son, Homer and Marge Simpson agree to Bart trialling a 'radical, untested and potentially dangerous' drug called 'Focusyn'. We see him morph in front of our eyes, moving from delinquent to angel to shivering paranoid wreck in double time. The episode closes with Homer and Marge deciding to take Bart off the drug trial, convinced that a mischievous Bart is better than a quiescent one.

Bart speaks the line in question at the midpoint of his story curve, as he reaches his short-lived zenith of manic politeness. He is sitting in class, listening to Mrs Krabappel talking about Wordsworth's 'Daffodils', when Nelson points out two dogs fighting in the playground. Everyone except Bart rushes to the window to watch. At which point he yells to his classmates to return to the lesson: ‘C’mon people, this poetry ain’t gonna appreciate itself’. It’s a brilliant joke, not just because we see Bart behaving out of character. It is also absurd, ridiculous. But I happen to think it is true. A poem is a dead thing until a person reads it, then, hopefully, shares it with someone else. Poems do not appreciate themselves. For that we need someone, as Thomas Lux puts it, to love it ‘enough to make you love it’. This book is my way of saying thank you to the people who have shared that love with me.

ANTHONY WILSON

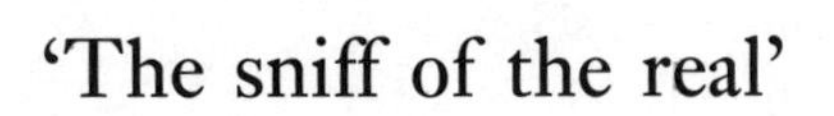
'The sniff of the real'

Autobiography

The sniff of the real, that's
what I'd want to get
            how it felt
to sit on Parliament
Hill on a May evening
studying for exams   skinny
seventeen   dissatisfied
            yet sniffing such
a potent air, smell of
grass in heat from
the day's sun

I'd been walking through the damp
rich ways by the ponds
and now lay on the upper
grass with Lamartine's poems

life seemed all
loss, and what was more
I'd lost whatever it was
before I'd even had it

a green dry prospect
distant babble of children
and beyond, distinct at
the end of the glow
St Paul's like a stone thimble

longing so hard to make
inclusions that the longing
has become   in memory
an inclusion

THOM GUNN
Collected Poems (Faber & Faber, 1994)

■ Thom Gunn's 'Autobiography', along with Norman MacCaig's 'Aunt Julia', was among the first poems I can remember placing myself at the centre of as I read it.

I can remember a little depth-charge of a tremor going off in my brain on encountering Ted Hughes's 'The Retired Colonel' in an English lesson at school, but this was something altogether new and exciting. The book we were reading was Geoffrey Summerfield's Penguin anthology *Worlds: Seven Modern Poets* (1974).

The experience of reading the book as a whole represents to me now something of a watershed: real money had changed hands for it, the first time I had invested, literally and otherwise, in a book. I was seventeen at the time, exactly the age of the speaker in Gunn's poem.

Looking back at it now, I suppose I understood half of *Worlds*, took in less of it, but comprehensively fell in love with all of it. I have no doubt that from the moment I first read it, I absolutely felt 'Autobiography' was written just for me.

I loved finding myself mirrored in lines which looked simultaneously casual and minimal. The seductive repetitive 's' sounds in 'studying for exams   skinny / seventeen   dissatisfied' echo those in the poem's two instances of the verb 'sniffing', from the first and eighth lines, the former a search for the 'real' and the latter luxuriating in potency.

I loved the psalm-like purity of the poem's gorgeous phrase-making: 'grass in heat from / the day's sun'; 'damp / rich ways by the ponds'; 'green dry prospect'; 'distant babble of children'.

Finally, and most of all I think, I loved that this was a voice from outside of the centre of London. Having grown up in its suburbs, my views of the great city had always been from a distance and protected. Here was a voice that paid homage both to being on the edge of things while clearly desperate to get to the centre. The adolescent nod to the world of children is freighted with both longing and the knowledge of not returning. The need for guidance into the adult world comes in the guise not of parents or teachers but in the form of a book of poems, which is explicitly read in solitude on 'upper' grass, with the world as it were at the feet of the speaker.

Yet this version of adolescence sings no notes of triumphalism. The words 'longing' and 'inclusion' are both used four times in the poem's final Carlos Williams-like stanza. In the words of Ted Hughes's 'October Dawn', you feel that everything is about to start, but not before the memory, and the effort of making it, have been recorded.

Tides

The evening advances, then withdraws again
Leaving our cups and books like islands on the floor.
We are drifting you and I,
As far from one another as the young heroes
Of these two novels we have just laid down.
For that is happiness: to wander alone
Surrounded by the same moon, whose tides remind us of ourselves,
Our distances, and what we leave behind.
The lamp left on, the curtains letting in the light.
These things were promises. No doubt we will come back to them.

HUGO WILLIAMS

Collected Poems (Faber & Faber, 2002)

■ I can remember exactly where I was when I first read this poem. It was on the balcony of the squat of my friend Duncan Kramer, in Bromley in the summer of 1984.

The house had been earmarked for demolition to make way for a ring road. It was shared by Duncan with five other art students, each of whom attended Ravensbourne College of Art on furniture/product and graphic design courses. It was perhaps the most chaotic house I had ever seen, with bikes and car repair tools littering the hallways and landing, no locks on the bathroom or lavatory doors (you had to claim occupancy with a post-it note), and a constant mix of music seeping through the pores of each floor and ceiling.

I used to escape my bedsit in Golders Green to visit Duncan on the other side of the universe, turning up at his door unannounced with a bottle of wine in the hope of being fed and entertained for the weekend. If he was irritated by these raids of mine, he never showed it.

I do think they were some of the most formative experiences of my life.

It was through Duncan that I had first met the work of Seamus Heaney (one winter he walked around with a copy of *Field Work* in his donkey jacket pocket), and now I was meeting other poets who were not on the syllabus of the English Literature degree I was doing: Paul Muldoon, Tom Paulin, Douglas Dunn, Michael Longley, Derek Mahon and Hugo Williams. They were all to be found between the pages of a tiny looking paperback, *The Penguin Book of Contemporary British Poetry*, edited by Blake Morrison and Andrew Motion and published only two years previously.

We were sitting on his balcony with coffee and the papers, having got up late one Saturday morning, when I began glancing through this little book of poems, intrigued by the artwork on the front cover and drawn in by the lure of reading more Heaney.

To the sound of weekend shopping and ordinary south London traffic I read these lines of quiet longing and utter clarity, feeling as though someone had taken a look inside my head and made a snapshot of it for all to see.

It seemed to describe perfectly the liminal world I was living in, with its descriptions of abandoned paperbacks, lamps left on and aimless wandering. I loved that I could see everything in the poem, while feeling that its main action as it were, remained mysterious, out of reach. Right at the poem's centre was a big abstract noun, 'happiness', a word I was deeply suspicious of, let alone seeing it described with such stark negatives, in terms of distances, departures and delayed fulfilment of promises.

Yet I was very happy to read it. My reading up to that point had been Geoffrey Summerfield's *Worlds* and A. Alvarez's *The New Poetry*, Hopkins and Plath for 'A' Level, Ted Hughes and McGough for 'O' Level, the early poems of T.S. Eliot, bits of Yevtushenko and some Thom Gunn. Having read Plath in particular, I was both surprised and delighted to see that the moon could appear just as itself.

It seems so obvious, looking back at it now, but I cannot overestimate the shock and the joy of discovering the power of plain language, aged 20, one sunny South London Saturday.

I have felt indebted to Duncan ever since that moment, for the frenzy of reading, borrowing, buying and writing of poetry that has ensued in my life as a result. I am not sure anything has come close, before or since, to confirming my pleasure in and awareness of the numinous, and awakening my desire to 'credit marvels' (Heaney again) in the everyday.

An Upstairs Kitchen

It is strange to that I used to think
The summers were best in this kitchen
High in the back of the house:
A time when thick greens
From the trees and the park beyond
Smother the windows
And enter the room.

A time when I easily leave the peeling
Or cleaning to drift and lean
On cool glass, drawn
By the astonishing pink of the jay,
By short bare legs which distantly
Lift the swings, by the dog
Racing the trains.

Strange, because now is clearly the time
I like best. The Bank Holiday fairs
Crammed close round the oaks
Have all gone; old ginger leaves
Are heaped soaking and deep in their place,
And the footballers' turkey-red shirts
Flare through the branches.

And some days, on the top edge of the far
Distance, through bare trees,
I can see the tower of the riverside
Church, where a mother lies
Buried with six of her children,
Three of them drowned
At different times.

How surprised she might be to know
That more than a century later
I worry in winters
Over her carelessness and pain,
While the iron gently noses its way
Between buttons and pleats
With soft steam sighs.

SUSANNAH AMOORE
Poetry Introduction 6 (Faber & Faber, 1985)

■ I first came across this poem in Faber's *Poetry Introduction 6.*

I found the book during my final year at university, at a time when I had just started buying books of poems for myself but with no idea of who to read, who was good, in or out. I plunged in, following my nose, badly. My copy of *Poetry Introduction 6* cost £3.95. Would that publishers could still make books that cheaply.

A bit of context. Faber and Faber were in their flock wallpaper design period, all those tiny interlocking ffs like some weird prediction of what we all now take for granted on Twitter. I had started writing poems, and had even showed them to a few brave friends, but had no idea how to get published or connected to the world of publishing. Every one of the poets in *Poetry Introduction 6* appeared to me to have arrived. I hoped some of that would rub off on me, just by owning the book.

I am not (and was not) a complicated reader. It was not complicated. In my clumsy and still adolescent way I ruthlessly placed myself at the centre of every poem I read.

Susannah Amoore is the first poet in the book. Poem 1, page 13, is called 'Long Sight'. As gangsters and cops say in *CSI Miami*: I am listening. It begins:

> If I squint
> I can nearly see myself now
> As I was in that
> Childhood-like summer of '71:

The poem as act of remembrance, as childhood reminiscence, sepia photograph, as 'blurred Liberty print'. I liked that. Keep it coming, I thought, this is what I know, this is what I want to do, yes.

Poem 2, 'At the End of April', page 14, contains a description of a cricket wicket being prepared. What was there not to like? Poem 3, 'Dawn in West Hampstead', page 15, is about breast-feeding. In West Hampstead. But wait. It is hard to overestimate the effect that proper noun had on me.

One, it meant you could use "real places" in poems, i.e. places which weren't really that poetic. (I had once tried to write a song about the Nautilus chip shop in West Hampstead. It was a disaster.) Two, I saw you could trust your reader. You did not need to put an asterisk at the bottom of the page saying 'West Hampstead is a not very exciting suburb of North West London, to the south of Hampstead.' Three, and most exciting of all, it meant we were practically neighbours!

Slowly, and badly, I was learning that you could put stuff in poems which were ordinary. Parks. Trees. Bowling greens. Stuff no one else was looking at, places no one else went but which were now special because just one person had stopped to look. Bamburgh beach. West Hampstead.

Poem 8, page 20, was called 'An Upstairs Kitchen'. The chaotic student house I was living in also had such a room, also 'high in the back of the house'. By now I thought Susannah Amoore had a hotline into my head. And by now you know I was in the habit of connecting as much of my life as possible to the world of the poems I came across. Like Amoore's, my kitchen had a view of trees, a park; and like Amoore, I had been known to 'easily leave the peeling / Or cleaning to drift and lean / On cool glass'.

Her work can be described as "delicate-domestic". Each of her poems contains knock-out lines and phrases which expand their humble origins: rooms 'lamp-lit by tea time'; 'bulky young birds teetering on the edge of / Flight'; 'The North Sea / Waits on the left, wickedly grey and cold, / Experienced at fingering wrecks, / Smoothing bones.'

I should have written to say thank you. Maybe I just have.

Instructor

This is the best bit; the steep glide into Milnsbridge,
the tight swing under the arch before the home straight,
when I'm behind the wheel, in the last minutes of my hour
and he's there, foot well clear of the brake, mumbling
into his mobile or reaching past me for his medicine.

Twenty-odd years in the Force, he knows about sensors
and patrols, so we sail through the ambers and reds
up to the Cowlersley crossroads. Outside the pub
two constables pause and turn on the pavement to salute us.
A stickler for politeness, he says, 'Wave back. Don't smile.'

I file it under pertinent advice:
never trust another bloke's indicators,
all dogs are unpredictable and ruthless,
know what the real speed limits are,
three ways to recognise an unmarked car.

ANN SANSOM
In Praise of Men and Other People (Bloodaxe Books, 2003)

■ Ann Sansom is one of my all-time favourite people, poets or normal, ever. I count myself fortunate to have worked with her on a number of occasions, not least because she is a fantastic professional who models patience, dialogue and enquiry in everything she says and does.

I am still learning from the way she turns diverting anecdote into profound instructions for writing and for life in her writing workshops: 'The best time to write is when you are tired; your conscious mind is less interfering then.' Or: 'See if you can finish a draft of a poem in the time it takes to run a bath.' I see these remarks as more of a life-raft than a touchstone. I have lost count of the times they have kept me afloat in dark times.

Sometimes, just as you are starting to write, Ann will say: 'It is not a competition'; 'No one is reading this'; or: 'You can't do it wrong.' People often ask her if it is OK to ignore the constraints of the exercise she has just set up. 'Of course it is. Rules are there to be broken. But it will give you a different poem.'

One day she turned up to a workshop with a slim volume of her poems in her hand. 'This is for you,' she said without ceremony, and began teaching. The book was a pamphlet called *Vehicle* (Slow Dancer, 1999). I loved it instantly, sneaking quick readings of poems between exercises. It contains descriptions of things that are fantastically hard to do well: cats, dogs, unemployment, train stations. It has the most beautiful poem about and for one of my other heroes, Michael Laskey. All of it feels natural and utterly controlled.

For some reason, though, 'Instructor' is the poem from *Vehicle* that really got to me. It is a microcosm of everything Ann does so well, in poem after poem, here and in all her books: beginning in medias res, no flag waving or signposting from behind the poem, just jump straight in. There is trust in the reader. You see it in her use of proper nouns (Milnsbridge, Cowlersley), the one line of dialogue ('Wave back. Don't smile.') which gives a whole life, the eye for the killer detail ('reaching past me for his medicine').

I wish, I wish, I wish Ann Sansom published more.

Slaughterhouse

Let it be done here, here where death
is all in a day's work, and by men who deal
in the thing itself. Spare me a slow decline,
years of pain and pills, months in bed,
weeks of too few visits, then too many.

Instead, give me a brief and rollicking ride
through Devon lanes, sun striating my face,
a gentle nudge out of the truck and into the gates
of the cattle race, the open arms of the crush
and the captive bolt's blind kiss.

Roll me over the grid in the next room
into the warm and expert hands of these,
the last men on earth to hold me; men skilled
in the precise and subtle use of knives,
the exercise of necessary force.

Then winch me through to where the others hang,
trimmed and tagged, bumping haunch to haunch,
couched in the companionable chill.

HILARY MENOS
Berg (Seren, 2009)

■ One of the most useful things I have done in my life was being a member of a group of poets who met to workshop each other's poems, from 2003 to 2005.

Every five weeks or so the poets in the group would meet in my kitchen over coffee and Danish to discuss poems which we were drafting. Each writer would read out their poem and then listen, in silence, while the rest of us made observations, comments and criticisms. Only when the rest of us had finished were authors allowed to respond. The format never changed.

Rather grandly, we called ourselves the South West Writers Group. The group comprised serious poetic talent and range, namely: Andy Brown, Ann Gray, Candy Neubert, Christopher Southgate, Hilary Menos and Julie-ann Rowell. The purpose was not to become like each other, but to enable us to become more like ourselves. Julie-ann writes differently from Ann and from Candy, who in turn is different from Hilary. There is room for all of us.

I first read 'Slaughterhouse' at my kitchen table, in the company of these great people. There is always a special kind of hush, filled with nervousness and expectation, that descends as a new poem is brought to the table. In the cases of poems as rare and exciting as 'Slaughterhouse' it is especially freighted with anticipation. Memory being what it is, this is far from reliable, but I think it may have been one of the especially rare poems from that time that we did not want to see changed at all.

What I love about the poem is the way it moves from warmth to coldness without ever raising its voice above a tone of voice which is closer to the intimate whispering of secrets across a pillow than it is the finality of a last will and testament.

I take great pleasure from the poem's plain diction spiced with words like 'rollicking' and 'striating'. I love the singsong music of 'nudge', 'truck' and 'crush'; and 'face', 'gates' and 'race' masking the 'necessary force' and logic of the poem's grim subject-matter. There are also great phrases here: 'the captive bolt's blind kiss'; 'the precise and subtle use of knives'; 'couched in the companionable chill'.

I find the latter especially arresting, for it seems a summary of how the poem has created its effects upon the reader. For one thing, 'couched in the companionable chill' is extremely difficult to say out loud. It is as though the clot it creates in the throat mimics in the body the slow realisation to the mind of the finality of its setting.

And what brilliantly odd words they are to put together. 'Couched' has a sense of something being put to bed, and of carrying extra meaning. 'Companionable' and 'chill' bounce off each other, rather like the carcasses the poem describes, each echoing the other's 'i' and 'l' sounds, but incompletely, reminding us that however satisfyingly the poem might serve up its pleasures, it can inevitably end only one way.

Caring for the Environment

In Wonderland, they say 'Drink Me'
but in Leeds they shoulder the bin aside
saying 'Take me to the bottle bank'
and leave stubborn rings on the lino
like 'We Woz 'Ere' graffiti,
reminding us how much wine
we get through in a week.

Once in the bag they shift and clack,
ageing the plastic with their weight and bulk,
melting the handles.
Five green wine, one gin and two big coffee jars.
Why is it always me who takes them back?
You're the bloody vegetarian.

But the task brings its own rewards.
Under the bright clatter, a tiny crunch
more like a subtext of things to come.
Something has engaged –
the last of those cheap wine glasses you bought.
I joggle the bag bloodthirstily.

The crash when the bank is full
or half-full, that's the best.
Is this really legal? But the thick rubber lips
reassure with their resistance.
Like bouncers at a nightclub
they can only be pushed so far.
This is a safe idea, a foolproof operation.

It's different when the bank is empty.
The stubborn ones will bounce like echoes
giving you the sense that something's gone off half-cock.

You peer after them helplessly.
Inside it's like a beer tent.

Outside the job's finished
with nothing left to do but bin the bag.
I bin the bag. A cough mixture bottle
has left its last secretions on my hands.
The steering wheel is sticky for days.

MANDY SUTTER
Poetry Business Anthology 1992: Greek Gifts (Smith/Doorstop, 1992)

■ In 1991 I made the decision to spend more of my time concentrating on the thing that fulfilled me the most, writing poems. To make this happen I began working part-time so that I could block off a part of each week in the pursuit of this.

I made several mistakes. If I had my time again I would have attended at least one Arvon course, mostly to meet other people. I would have gone to more poetry readings. I would have written more.

One thing I do not look back on with any regret is the amount of reading I did. Subscribing to as many poetry magazines as I could, I read, I felt, everything I could get my hands on, aware at the same time that I was barely scratching the surface of what was available.

The twin achievements of this intense phase of reading and writing were that (a) I wrote a lot of poems – some good, most of them bad, but all of them mine; and (b) I felt more alive and less alone at the end than I did at the beginning. (I still often wonder if the latter is not the chief purpose of all of my writing, for better or worse.)

When I am asked for it, the advice I most often repeat is: *read.* To write poetry, you need to be in relationship with poetry. It is not rocket science. But it is a process, and you do need to commit to it. One of the best ways of feeling less alone is to subscribe to poetry magazines. (Or there is Arvon.) You realise there are other people out there who are just as afflicted with poetry as you are. And you can learn from them, guess at their influences, watch them develop, even write to them.

Not long after I made the decision I mention above, a poem of mine was chosen for an anthology called *Greek Gifts, the Poetry Business Competition Anthology of 1992*. Having a poem taken notice of in this way was exciting enough. But what really thrilled me was the sudden and intoxicating feeling of being part of a group of people. I have gone on to meet some of writers in the book, but most I have never met. You may recognise them because they are still faithful to their calling of writing poems: Martyn Crucefix, Jane Draycott, Jane Duran, Sue Hubbard, Christopher North, Ruth Padel, Mandy Sutter, Tamar Yoseloff.

The poem from this anthology which jumped out at me most immediately is one about that most ordinary of domestic tasks, the trip to the bottle bank.

Mandy Sutter's poem is a delight to me because it achieves what would take prose so much longer to spell out, comment upon and then reinforce. I do not think there is much in it which needs explicating.

But I do love and admire the way the poem has something at stake, albeit a Big Theme (the environment) under the cloak of an everyday incident, carrying it into our hearts as it were through the power of story. I like the way it is addressed to a 'you', invisibly drawing the reader in and making them complicit with the poem's assumptions. Most of all I relish the poem's economy. 'You're the bloody vegetarian' possesses both charm and wit: a novel would take pages to uncover the tensions merely hinted at here.

'Caring for the Environment' saved my life by saying 'Yes, this is what it's like', at a moment when I needed the next spur to carry on writing. I think I would give my arm to have written the line, 'Inside it's like a beer tent'.

It is not a famous poem. It is not in a famous anthology. This is precisely the point.

Domestic Bliss

The mess gets worse as the beautiful world
tries harder, expands on its original mistake –
something crass blurted out in a fluster –
making a mountain out of moleshit.

You and I aren't bothered. Too busy to
beat the wolves back from the doorstep, too tired
to be pissed off at anything, tonight
the blackcurrant wine is dyeing our tongues

the colour of our hearts. We're saying what we mean,
for once, and it feels good, making plans
for the future as if there were no tomorrow.
Your smile leaps out from behind your teeth.

We can do whatever we want.
What we want to do right now is
get sordid in front of the fire.
The world is hard but worth it.

MARK ROBINSON

How I Learned to Sing: New & Selected Poems (Smokestack Books, 2013) by permission of the author.

■ 'Domestic Bliss' saved my life at a time that was incredibly exciting for me, around 1991. I had just rearranged my working life around reading and writing poetry, part of which process meant I had begun subscribing to a range of small press poetry magazines which were new to me. *Scratch* was one of these.

Also around this time I began running a writers and artists group called Bull, with my friend Luke Bretherton, in my kitchen in Brixton. For the price of a bottle of (usually very cheap red) wine, friends of friends of friends could descend on our house and read/ show/play their latest piece of work. As I say, all of this was new and exciting to me.

Up until this point I had written alone, in the dark and in secret. It had taken me a very long time to notice that no one knew my work because I was not showing it to anyone. Subscribing to magazines like *Scratch* and taking part in Bull were among the most the most formative experiences of my writing life, therefore. Suddenly I was in contact with people who cared about words and poems and metaphors in the same way I did. I realised I was not alone.

So I would send Mark my wry little poems about changing nappies and I would see his in *Scratch* and in other places like *The North* and *The Wide Skirt*. I liked them immediately because, as Kenneth Koch said about Frank O'Hara, there was nothing in them I did not like. There were references to the music of Motown and making curry, all shot through with a gentle cynicism which never overwhelmed the poems or threatened to become less than generous.

I love 'Domestic Bliss' because it reminds me of that time and because it is a lovely domestic poem that achieves much more than it appears to do, all in the space of 16 lines (or a glass of blackcurrant wine). I do think you would have to be from Mars not to be able to relate to what it describes. On a personal note I want to say that 'The world is hard but worth it' is one of the great last lines of any poem, and I wish I had written it.

'Your smile leaps out from behind your teeth' is not far behind.

Saint Francis and the Sow

The bud
stands for all things,
even for those things that don't flower,
for everything flowers, from within, of self-blessing;
though sometimes it is necessary
to reteach a thing its loveliness,
to put a hand on its brow
of the flower
and retell it in words and in touch
it is lovely
until it flowers again from within, of self-blessing;
as Saint Francis
put his hand on the creased forehead
of the sow, and told her in words and in touch
blessings of earth on the sow, and the sow
began remembering all down her thick length,
from the earthen snout all the way
through the fodder and slops to the spiritual curl of the tail,
from the hard spininess spiked out from the spine
down through the great broken heart
to the sheer blue milken dreaminess spurting and shuddering
from the fourteen teats into the fourteen mouths sucking and
          blowing beneath them:
the long, perfect loveliness of sow.

GALWAY KINNELL
Selected Poems (Houghton Mifflin, USA; Bloodaxe Books, UK, 2001)

■ Seamus Heaney describes the kind of religious, 'conspiratorial' hush about being shown a well-loved poem for the first time. At once private and communal, it seems to reach into spaces we all carry that are non-verbal, or pretty much that way for most of the time. I was first shown 'Saint Francis and the Sow' in much the way Heaney describes, by Jean Sprackland at the Arvon Foundation's writing centre at Totleigh Barton.

That week we had given our group a pre-course task, of bringing to the course one book of poems they felt passionate about, to share and discuss with others. Jean brought Kinnell's Bloodaxe *Selected*. I had not seen it or the poem before.

My initial reaction to it was one of surprise and great fondness. I loved that it dared to hymn unlovely subject-matter. I loved its complete self-absorption in the living moment of description. I loved that it did not seem to care a hoot what I thought about it.

Reading it again now, I think daring is not far from the mark. It seems to take two very distinct strains of American poetry, beginning in didacticism and ending with tender praise, and blends them without one overshadowing the other. That is both risky and skilful. Poems that do that usually fall flat on their backsides, while this one achieves lift-off and in plain sight.

But it is in more than admiration that I come to this poem. It is "about" a sow, and the sowiness of sows, returning us the earthy facts of the matter with both precision and exultation. I happen to think it is just as much about teaching and suffering, and the counter-cultural energy that is released when we choose to utter praise. As one of our group said at the time, the poem enacts its own meaning, flowering into 'self-blessing' like the 'bud' it describes, in spite of its 'broken heart' and 'creased forehead'.

If that is not a miracle, I don't know what is.

Things I Learned at University

How to bike on cobblestones and where to signal right.
How to walk through doors held by Old Etonians
and not scowl. How to make myself invisible in seminars
by staring at the table. How to tell Victorian Gothic from Medieval.
How to eat a Mars bar in the Bodleian. when to agree
with everything in theory. How to cultivate a taste for sherry.

Where to bike on the pavement after dark. How to sabotage a hunt.
When to sunbathe topless in the Deer Park. When to punt.
How to hitch a lift and when to walk and where to run.
When not to address my tutors formally. How to laugh at Latin puns
and when to keep quiet and preserve my integrity.
How to celebrate an essay crisis. When to sleep through fire alarms.

How to bike no-handed, how to slip a condom on with one.
When to smoke a joint and when to swig champagne.
When to pool a tip and how to pull a pint. A bit of history.
When to listen to friends and whether to take them seriously.
At the same time how to scorn tradition and enjoy it.
How to live like a king, quite happily, in debt.

KATE BINGHAM
Cohabitation (Seren, 1998)

■ I found 'Things I Learned at University' in a pile of books on a table at the Arvon Foundation. Browsing without a great deal of expectation, it was doubly welcome to come across work so alive and witty. Furthermore, I had the strong sensation that it was a good deal more serious than it pretended to be. I read it cover to cover in one go.

The wit of 'Things I Learned at University' is twofold. From the use of the past tense in the title we learn that the person writing the poem is not the person doing the learning, but a person writing about another person. The magic shift in perspective created by hindsight allows experience to be presented, without commentary, with wry and affectionate summary.

Secondly, the poem is playful with the notion of what constitutes 'learning'. The only formal education mentioned in the poem is 'a bit of history'. All other knowledge is to be gleaned from a gentle subversion of that old cliché the university of life: pulling pints, cycling on pavements, living in debt etc. In the poem's own terms, it neatly scorns tradition while enjoying it. Think how different the poem's tone would be (and the reader's response to it) had it been called 'Things I Learned at Oxford'.

Formally the poem appears to grow more conscious of itself the longer it goes on. I relished the buried half-rhymes of 'Etonian', 'Victorian' and 'Bodleian'; of 'theory', 'sherry', and 'agree'. Linking these words in sound is only half the fun: repeated in list form they start to create dynamic whorls of nonsensical association, beloved by the surrealists and student drinking-games. Which is perhaps the point.

I savour, too, the looping rhymes in the second and third stanza: 'run' and 'puns' with 'one'; 'integrity' with 'history' and 'seriously'. The seriousness of the poem can be found in these formal pleasures, but it is there, too, in knowing 'when to keep quiet', becoming 'invisible' in seminars, and 'when not to address my tutors formally'. These moments are about confidence, identity and language, of learning to use them in order to fit in, the growing awareness of the catastrophe of using them with the wrong people, or at the wrong time.

Like all great poems, all of this learning is worn lightly. It comes to us in the form of a list. It might have been dashed off during an 'essay crisis' or while rolling a joint. It gives the impression of not being the real thing at all. Deep down it knows that it is.

Timetable

We all remember school, of course:
the lino warming, shoe bag smell, expanse
of polished floor. It's where we learned
to wait: hot cheeked in class, dreaming,
bored, for cheesy milk, for noisy now.
We learned to count, to rule off days,
and pattern time in coloured squares:
purple English, dark green Maths.

We hear the bells, sometimes,
for years, the squeal and crack
of chalk on black. We walk, don't run,
in awkward pairs, hoping for the open door,
a foreign teacher, fire drill. And love
is long aertex summers, tennis sweat,
and somewhere, someone singing flat.
The art room, empty, full of light.

KATE CLANCHY
Slattern (Picador, 1995)

I first read 'Timetable' in the *Times Educational Supplement* in the early 90s. I was sitting in a primary school staffroom, on a coffee break.

The poem was part of a feature-length article and interview with Kate Clanchy, the main construct of which seemed to be her 'progression' from school teacher to poet. It was absolutely clear from the first word, both article and poem, that this was a person who knew exactly what she was doing.

At the time I had been sending out poems to magazines, doing the odd reading and open mike, and trying to feel less alone in my quest to get a book out into the world. The poem in front of me fused perfectly both the world I was sitting in and the one I wanted to enter. The recognition was sudden and delicious. I took it as a sign.

I loved the poem's plain diction ('We all remember school'; 'It's where we learned / to wait'; 'We learned to count'), seduced at the same time by 'dreaming, / bored' and the longing contained in 'hoping for the open door'. I wanted to say to the poem: 'How did you know? That's me exactly!' The possible worlds on offer felt tantalisingly within in reach.

Looking at the poem again now, all these years later, I am struck again by the deliberate placing of key words on line-ends: 'expanse', 'dreaming', 'now', 'crack', 'run', 'door', 'love', 'sweat', 'light'. The plainness, even the flatness, of the some of the lines leads thrillingly towards these moments which open the poem up beyond recall and into vision.

'Ordinariness renewed'

Night Drive

The smells of ordinariness
Were new on the night drive through France;
Rain and hay and woods on the air
Made warm draughts in the open car.

Signposts whitened relentlessly.
Montrueil, Abbéville, Beauvais
Were promised, promised, came and went,
Each place granting its name's fulfilment.

A combine groaning its way late
Bled seeds across its work-light.
A forest fire smouldered out.
One by one small cafés shut.

I thought of you continuously
A thousand miles south where Italy
Laid its loin to France on the darkened sphere.
Your ordinariness was renewed there.

SEAMUS HEANEY
Opened Ground: Poems 1966-1996 (Faber & Faber, 2002)

■ 'Night Drive' is not especially famous or noteworthy, but I love it. It reminds me of the holidays, and poetry should always be the holidays.

It explores in a resolutely low-key register those fertile and liminal spaces between wakefulness and sleep, light and dark, arrival and departure. As in so many of Heaney's poems, there is a back-note of cautionary guilt and self-reproach running across the lines; the separation which causes the poem to be written is celebrated as it appears to be mourned.

A masterclass in how to write about nothing much at all, the poem is bookended in its first and final lines by the word 'ordinariness'. Some years after he wrote it, Heaney used the word 'gunslinger' to describe the approach of his poem 'Digging'.

Below the tactful surface of 'Night Drive' it is possible to detect something of that same bravado, albeit a quieter one: in the suggestive and repetitive 'l' sounds of 'smells', 'relentlessly', 'Montreuil', 'Abbéville' and 'fulfilment' which deliberately and not-quite-discreetly set up a chime with Italy laying its loin to France.

The poem is much more than an exercise in delayed gratification, however. It asks the question so central to Heaney's work as a whole: how far is an artist ever fully present in their inhabited circumstances and therefore necessarily prey to the guile required to craft poetry from experience? Heaney would never resort to something so vulgar as an answer, but there is a hint in the poem's penultimate word 'renewed' of the speaker's belief in life as redemptive, even if it is qualified as ordinary and under the cover of darkness.

‘This morning was cold’

This morning was cold, but it warmed about midday.
Blue clouds piled up in the north.
I came from a meeting – a discussion of
the teaching of classical languages –
and I was sitting by the river with a friend
who wanted to tell me his troubles.
The water was still high. Two boys
were throwing pebbles from the bank into the river.
I had no counsel to offer.... There were
no benches on the bank – probably night vandals
had thrown them into the water once again.
The sun slipped behind a cloud. We were freezing.
We rose and went back to town.
Perhaps he could see his course.
I stopped at a shop for oatmeal and bread.
It was June. Going home, I saw
three young militiamen winding their Rubik’s cube.

JAAN KAPLINSKI

translated from the Estonian by Jaan Kaplinski
with Sam Hamill and Riina Tamm

The Wandering Border (Harvill, 1992), by permission of the author.

■ Some poets you discover on your own, following your nose, not really knowing what you are up to. One of these is the work of the Estonian scholar, politician and poet Jaan Kaplinski. I try to read something by him on most days; increasingly I am thinking of him as my desert island poet, the one I would keep above all others. I can't really explain this any more rationally than to say I just like being in his presence. That's it.

Reading his poems I feel as though he is sitting across the room/table/chair from me, silently nodding or smiling. As Philip Gross said in his seminal early review of his work 'Very conscious of the places words cannot reach, his poems create a space around them that is intensely good to be in.' That pretty much sums it up for me.

It reminds me of an Ethan Canin quote in Anne Lamott's *Bird by Bird*. He says the most important thing a storyteller needs is a narrative voice the reader will find likeable. Kaplinski possesses this.

The poem opposite is from my favourite of his books, *The Wandering Border* (1992), translated into beautiful plain English. I should say at this point that it is not included in his recent and triumphant *Selected Poems* (Bloodaxe Books, 2011) – which you should buy anyway.

What I love about the poem is the way it presents an ordinary sequence of events as though they were at the same time full of mystery and even a little menace, but without any accompanying commentary or moralising. The speaker is explicit: 'I had no counsel to offer…' and this applies equally to the presence of 'night vandals', the 'freezing' June weather and 'militiamen', as well as the 'troubles' of his friend. The poem pulls back from seeking to be, in a phrase of Seamus Heaney's, 'instrumental or effective'. It is prepared to let things coexist, if not happily, then at least with clarity, allowing the speaker and world he is part of to 'see his course', implicitly inviting us to do the same.

Corminboeuf 157

I am writing these poems
As fast as I can

So that I don't miss out on my late style
Which will be extremely allusive,

Very simple,
Freer than anything I've ever done.

(The compromises will be different.)
When I get there, the work

Will be already changing,
Further from everything,

Although I don't want to say goodbye,
And yet closer,

As the saucer reminds us of the cup.
The things that are not mentioned

Will go on existing,
Exerting their unspeakable presence

Like childhood
Or the books beside the bed in the next room –

I have my Montagne Sainte-Victoire.
The poems will be the wonder of the future

And totally American
Like the work of all of the poets

From Eastern Iowa
Who live in Corminboeuf.

ROBERT REHDER

The Compromises Will Be Different (Carcanet Press, 1995)

■ Robert Rehder was from Iowa, educated at Princeton and lived for much of his life in Corminboeuf, a tiny hamlet in French-speaking Switzerland, which no one, not even the Swiss, have heard of.

His poems are an absolute delight, if you do not know his work. He published two collections with Carcanet, *The Compromises Will be Different* (1995) and *First Things When* (2009). I urge you to read him.

I discovered his work through a review of his first book by Ian McMillan. I seem to remember him saying there was something kind of Huddersfield and kind of New York in his work, mixed with kind of something else he could not put his finger on.

Labels are always a bad place to start when discussing poetry, a topic Rehder wrote much about in his academic work (when people ask me what kind of poetry I write I say 'The good kind, of course!'), but as it happens McMillan was onto something, particularly the thing he could not put his finger on.

Mark Halliday has a line in one of his essays about contemporary poetry making intense investigations into ever smaller units of experience (I paraphrase). This seems to me much of what Rehder was up to. The effect is self-deprecating and charming.

A Rehder poem is often about nothing very much at all: 'I am so bored by Corminboeuf / That I can't stand it – // My boredom, that is. / I like Corminboeuf. // Only about half a dozen times a day / I wish I was somewhere else' ('Corminboeuf XXXIX').

When nothing dries up there is always the subject of the poems' composition to write about. I am still not sure if Rehder chose to do this as an act of defiance or desperation. 'I have just composed the first / Corminboeuf poem.// If this doesn't put Corminboeuf on the map,/ What will?' ('The Affidavit [Corminboeuf II]').

Writing in a foreign country in the middle of nowhere seems to have energised Rehder hugely. The poems in *First Things When* are still about themselves, about nothing and about Corminboeuf, sometimes simultaneously, sometimes as if they each represent one another. But there is wonderful satire on the America of George W. Bush and on mall-culture, too. It is darker, perhaps, and tinged with sadness.

Bike

You, who have borne three sons
of mine, still bear my weight
routinely, transporting me.

An odd pair: your classic spare
lines – elbows, bony frame –
and me, bearlike, cumbersome,

nosing tangled coils of air
you cut through with your pure
purposeful geometry.

With you it's feet off the ground,
a feat passing unremarked
though in full public view.

Keeping each other's balance.
Our talk slow recurrent clicks,
companionable creaks.

Through you I've come to know
winds inside out and raw
weather ignored before;

and nuances of slopes,
the moving earth, green tracks
for blackberries and sloes

for gin, for jam: the tug
and tang of fruit pulling me
clear of the wheel of myself.

MICHAEL LASKEY

The Tightrope Wedding (Smith/Doorstop Books, 1999)

■ Now that Britain has started to think of itself as the greatest cycling nation since dinosaurs roamed the earth it seems a good time to turn to those events in our lives which we perform daily and routinely and for which, as Miles Kington once memorably said, there are no gold medals: the moment when you run for a bus weighed down with shopping; or when you cycle to work, are delayed by a puncture, and still make it on time. Richard Ford called this 'the normal applauseless life'.

In the case of my hero Michael Laskey this relates specifically to living a good life that has immeasurably improved the quality of life and lives of poetry and poets in this country, and writing poetry of rare integrity and power.

Some time in 1999 Michael gave me his book of poems *The Tightrope Wedding* (Smith/Doorstop, 1999). This was a gift, pure and simple. I treasure it deeply. It contains poems about ratatouille, batting for England by the back door, home movies and sports days. One of the poems is called 'Small Town Life' and this might have served as an adequate summary of the book's concerns as a whole. But 'adequate' and 'small' are far from what a Michael Laskey poem is essentially about. The book takes its title (with a brilliant *tour de force* of a poem) from the photograph (photographer unknown): 'Couple in Wedding Dress on Tightrope'. From an image that records both recklessness and simplicity and which we have now grown used to misnaming 'surreal', Laskey celebrates the daring in the everyday.

'Bike' is a perfect example of what Michael Laskey is up to in poem after poem in *The Tightrope Wedding*. He makes the ordinary seem strange, and reinvents 'routine' experience as potentially pregnant with mystery. I do think the poem is up there with that other great poem of the bicycle, Seamus Heaney's 'Wheels Within Wheels', which explicitly makes a link between pedal pushing and writing poetry in the phrase 'an access of free power'.

Laskey's poem, one of direct address to the bike in question, ends on a similar note of release as the speaker is pulled 'clear of the wheel of myself', the expectation of which is set up slyly and deftly in line 3. This may be the goal of all poems, to end in a place which is new from that which marked the starting out, the self and all its attendant concerns obliterated for a moment of self-forgetfulness, experienced paradoxically as one of completion.

Mansize

Now you aren't here I find
myself ironing linen squares,
three by three, the way
my mother's always done,
the steel tip steaming over your
blue initial. I, who resent
the very thought of this back-breaking
ritual, preferring radiator-dried
cottons, stiff as boards, any amount
of crease and crumple to this
soothing, time-snatching, chore.

I never understood my father's trick,
his spare for emergencies, but was glad
of its airing-cupboard comforts often enough:
burying my nose in it, drying my eyes
with it, staunching my blood with it,
stuffing my mouth with it. His expedience,
my mother's weekly art, leaves me
forever flawed: rushing into newsagents
for Kleenex, rifling your pockets in the cinema,
falling on those cheap printed florals,

when what I really want is Irish linen,
shaken out for me to sink my face in,
the shape and scent of you still warm
in it, your monogram in chainstitch
at the corner. Comforter, seducer, key witness
to it all, my neatly folded talisman,
my sweet flag of surrender.

MAURA DOOLEY

Sound Barrier: Poems 1982-2002 (Bloodaxe Books, 2002)

■ I first heard Maura Dooley's poem 'Mansize' on the radio. I was stuck in traffic at the time, in Tooting in south London. This was a very hectic time of life, in which the acts of reading, listening to, talking about and writing poems seemed every bit as important as getting my children dressed and fed each morning.

Seldom alone, in the car or anywhere else, I switched on the radio to listen to the old Radio 4 arts programme *Kaleidoscope*, as I crawled along. The announcer's voice cut straight to Maura's own reading 'Mansize' from her collection *Explaining Magnetism* (Bloodaxe Books, 1991).

I was struck immediately by the poem's intimate mode of address, speaking directly both to its subject and reader with apparent artless disregard for everything other than telling the truth. It is about much more than it is about: gender, age, history, resistance, language and freedom. But there isn't a word of it that is difficult. Like many of Maura's poems, it wields the most gentle of stilettos.

I think nowadays I could have ordered *Explaining Magnetism* on my Amazon app before reaching Balham. Back then I had to ring up an actual bookshop and spell the author's name and publisher to them on the phone, then wait two weeks, before I could hear it again.

In the words of John Logan's 'The Picnic' (see page 72), the poem entered my life at a moment when I was determined to be receptive to poems 'talk[ing] in another way I wanted to know'. This is what I mean by poems having the capacity to save lives: sitting on a sofa or stationary on the South Circular, once they enter you nothing is ever the same.

Mushrooms

Overnight, very
Whitely, discreetly,
Very quietly

Our toes, our noses
Take hold on the loam,
Acquire the air.

Nobody sees us,
Stops us, betrays us;
The small grains make room.

Soft fists insist on
Heaving the needles,
The leafy bedding,

Even the paving.
Our hammers, our rams,
Earless and eyeless,

Perfectly voiceless,
Widen the crannies,
Shoulder through holes. We

Diet on water,
On crumbs of shadow,
Bland-mannered, asking

Little or nothing.
So many of us!
So many of us!

We are shelves, we are
Tables, we are meek,
We are edible,

Nudgers and shovers
In spite of ourselves.
Our kind multiplies:

We shall by morning
Inherit the earth.
Our foot's in the door.

SYLVIA PLATH
Collected Poems (Faber & Faber, 1981/2002)

■ I think my first bout of Poetry Exhaustion occurred sometime after my 'A' Levels. Our English paper was quite advanced for its time (at least, we were told that it was). Alongside two Shakespeare plays and Chaucer's *Wife of Bath* we also had Hopkins, Stoppard's *Jumpers*, Faulkner's *As I Lay Dying* and Sylvia Plath's *Ariel*. That might look a bit staid now, what Ian McMillan calls 'twist and reek', but I think it changed my life.

In the way that we were instructed, perhaps because of the pressure of time, we worked through a selection of *Ariel* poems rather than the whole book. Among others we did: 'Morning Song', 'The Applicant', 'Lady Lazarus', 'Daddy', 'Fever 103°', 'The Moon and the Yew Tree', 'Stings', 'Balloons' and 'Edge'. I still have my copy of the book now. It contains phrases like 'utter failure' (next to the final stanza of 'The Arrival of the Bee Box') and 'beginning to doubt her own specialness' (next to 'Stings').

Do not tell me you have not done this too.

I remember asking for (and getting) the then newly published *Collected Poems* for my 18th birthday, just before the exams, and poring over Ted Hughes's Introduction, both marvelling at and puzzled by its restraint and lack of useful biographical information. Unprompted by any teacher I remember taking myself to the school library to find a book which contained an essay about Plath. It centred on poems which had been off piste for us: 'Cut', 'Nick and the Candlestick', 'The Night Dances' and 'You're'.

I was intrigued, because the poet that emerged from these pages was unlike anything I had encountered in lessons. The voice, self-dramatisation and stunning facility with words were recognisably Plath, but the setting and subject of the poems seemed more explicitly domestic than what I had come to believe was "real" Plath territory. That they were full of tenderness troubled me.

In the way that you do, I mugged up on these new discoveries, probably replacing old knowledge about the rest of the poems in the process. The exams came and went, as they do.

I did not look at the poems again for another two years. By this time I had progressed to studying them for an undergraduate degree. I am not exactly sure that 'progression' is what was taking place, however. Two key new ingredients had now come into play. We were directed towards a great deal of biographical information about Plath, in the form of speculation, especially regarding her marriage to Ted Hughes. Equally forceful was our professors' open dislike of Hughes and his work. (One of them suggested reading Philip Larkin's 'Horror Poet', his review of the *Collected Poems*. It is a decision I still regret.) While I had been dozing at the back, it felt as though territorial lines had been drawn up around interpretations of both poets' life and work, complete with trenches, supply networks and gun turrets.

Neutrality was not an option. I ducked and stumbled and hedged. I re-read my now useless 'A' Level notes and wished I was studying History. Though I knew I still loved the poems, I did not read Plath again for years.

A period of not very fruitful drifting followed. I worked for a small publishing firm for a while, then kind of collapsed. All this time I had been writing, as it were in the dark, knowing no other writers, but sensing there was a group of people out there to whom poems mattered as much as they did to me. Still living at home, I began working for a community arts project. For the first time I found myself going to, and then conducting, writing workshops. To my immense surprise, my colleagues were very encouraging about these. From percussion to drama to improvisation, I became emboldened by the way my fellow-practitioners would lead their own workshops. I noticed that they would often begin a session with the very briefest of outlines of what they wanted us to achieve. They seemed to possess an extraordinary capacity for letting things evolve, encouraging participants to think of their discoveries as though they had created them on their own.

Before long I found myself taking part in reminiscence workshops, in part scaffolded by the reading aloud of poems. This took place in a hospice in North London. I used to take along my copy of Seamus Heaney and Ted Hughes's *The Rattle Bag* and open it almost at random, like a poetry jukebox: 'John Clare? Who wants a bit of John Clare?' If no one did, we would choose something else.

One week I remember reading out Plath's 'Pheasant'. In particular I loved its dying fall of challenge and acceptance: 'let be, let be'. This triggered a memory of discovering, just prior to 'A' Levels, that "other" Plath of hushed, domestic tones and subdued hues. I wondered if there were others I had missed out on.

This is how I came across 'Mushrooms'. It may well have developed an afterlife as a "workshop poem" (I can think of at least two anthologies it appears in), but in those days it did not feel well-known at all. For a while it helped me subscribe to my batty binary theory that there were two Sylvia Plaths: one, the monster beloved of (some of) my university professors, and the other an ordinary woman staring in wonderment at every little thing.

It sent me back to my yellowing *Collected*. Nervously I found myself ditching my preconceived ideas. Even more tentatively I found myself nodding in agreement with Ted Hughes's view of Sylvia Plath as possessing an 'artisan-like' attitude towards writing poems: 'if she couldn't get a table out of the material, she was quite happy to get a chair, or even a toy'. Whatever else we know (or think we know) about Hughes, this practitioner's eye-view seems extraordinarily tender to me. I wished I'd paid attention to it when the book first arrived in my life as an under-appreciated gift, but a gift nevertheless.

My Shoes

Shoes, secret face of my inner life:
Two gaping toothless mouths,
Two partly decomposed animal skins
Smelling of mice-nests.

My brother and sister who died at birth
Continuing their existence in you,
Guiding my life
Toward their incomprehensible innocence.

What use are books to me
When in you it is possible to read
The Gospel of my life on earth
And still beyond, of things to come?

I want to proclaim the religion
I have devised for your perfect humility
And the strange church I am building
With you as the altar.

Ascetic and maternal, you endure:
Kin to oxen, to Saints, to condemned men,
With your mute patience, forming
The only true likeness of myself.

CHARLES SIMIC
Selected Poems 1963-2003 (Faber & Faber, 2004)

■ It was the best of times. Jean Sprackland and I were tutoring the dream group at Totleigh Barton for a week. As anyone who has done an Arvon course knows, the talk was all about writing poems, how we went about our writing, where our ideas came from, who we were reading and who we knew or had worked with. This went on pretty much continuously, over breakfast, coffee and dinner.

I said to one of the participants I am still in touch with that I am still learning from it several years later. This was not meant flippantly.

I remember the last workshop Jean gave, right at the end of the week, on four of Charles Simic's poems. I had read Simic before, in anthologies and had also come across him at workshops. Though I did not know why, I didn't really feel I had got him yet. Happily, Jean's workshop changed all that.

She handed out a photocopied sheet with four of Simic's poems on it, all taken from a back issue of the *LRB*. I still have my notes from the session. They say things like 'secret objects', 'personal', 'speed→cutting through' and 'everyday'. Looking at them from this distance, they have the shock of appearing as a kind of shorthand *ars poetica*.

Via Jean's careful explication I now felt I had access to Simic's strange merging of the language of religion ('inner life', 'Gospel', 'existence', 'humility', 'church', 'altar', 'patience' and 'Saints') with that of earth ('shoes', 'face', 'mouths', 'skins', 'mice', 'birth', 'earth', 'oxen'). The chiming assonance of several of these ('patience' with 'Saints'; 'shoes' with 'face' and 'mice'; 'birth' with 'earth') is persuasive and seductive.

'My Shoes' is also deeply political. In an era when we share the minutiae of 'inner lives', directly and indirectly making them available to all who would listen, Simic implicitly seems to argue for a core self which is irreducible and which cannot be known or "read".

I find this bizarrely hopeful.

The Black Wet

It's raining stair-rods and chairlegs,
it's raining candelabra and microwaves,
it's raining eyesockets.
When the sun shines through the shower
it's raining the hair of Sif,
each strand of which is real gold
(carat unknown).

It's raining jellyfish,
it's raining nuts, bolts and pineal glands,
it's raining a legion of fly noyades,
it's raining marsupials and echnidae,
it's raining anoraks in profusion.
It's siling, it's spittering, it's stotting, it's teeming,
it's pouring, it's snoring, it's plaining, it's Spaining.

People look up, open their mouths momentarily,
and drown.
People look out of windows and say,
'Send it down, David.'
Australians remark, 'Huey's missing the bowl.'
Americans reply, 'Huey, Dewie and Louie
are missing the bowl.'

It is not merely raining,
it's Windering and Thirling, it's Buttering down.
It's raining lakes, it's raining grass-snakes,
it's raining Bala, Baikal, and balalaikas,
it's raining soggy sidewinders and sadder adders.
It's raining flu bugs, Toby jugs and hearth-rugs,
it's raining vanity.

The sky is one vast water-clock
and it's raining seconds, it's raining years:
already you have spent more of your life looking at the rain
that you have sleeping, cooking, shopping and making love.
It's raining fusilli and capeletti,
it's raining mariners and albatrosses,
it's raining iambic pentameters.

Let's take a rain-check:
it's raining houndstooth and pinstripe,
it's raining tweed. This is the tartan of McRain.
This is the best test of the wettest west:
it is not raining locusts – just.
Why rain pests
when you can rain driving tests?

It is raining through the holes in God's string vest.

W.N. HERBERT
The Laurelude (Bloodaxe Books, 1998)

NOTE: *The black wet* (Scots) – rain as opposed to snow

■ In 2002 I heard W.N. Herbert read 'The Black Wet' at the Aldeburgh Poetry Festival. This is not remarkable in itself, you might say, and perhaps you would be right. The truly remarkable thing about Bill's reading is that I can still see and hear him delivering it all these years later. For someone with the attention span of a gnat, this is unusual.

It was a beautifully paced reading, with proper peaks and troughs, moments of slapstick comedy followed by lyrical grace; towering rage followed by barehanded grief. For me the stand-out moment was Bill's reading of 'The Black Wet'.

With Bill's performance still fresh in my mind's eye, I am reminded that on hearing it I spent most of the time laughing. 'How does he do that?' I remember thinking, as the poem swirled around us and gathered unstoppable momentum, seemingly bringing everything in the world into its unique force-field of upside down logic.

I see this poem as a kind of chant or spell, the better with which to curse and/or bless the generosity of the heavens. It is always a good day when you can mutter under your breath 'It's raining Bala, Baikal, and balalaikas, / it's raining soggysidewinders and sadder adders.'

I love the love of wordplay at the heart of this poem's enterprise. The energy it generates reminds me of those music hall entertainers spinning plates.

Nine years later everything is still in the air. Nothing has come crashing to earth yet.

Cups

They know us by our lips. They know the proverb
about the space between us. Many slip.
They are older than their flashy friends, the glasses.
They held cold water first, are named in scripture.

Most are gregarious. You'll often see them
nestled in snowy flocks on trestle tables
or perched on trolleys. Quite a few stay married
for life in their own home to the same saucer

and some are virgin brides of quietness
in a parlour cupboard, wearing gold and roses.
Handleless, chipped, some live on in the flour bin,
some with the poisons in the potting shed.

Shattered, they lie in flowerpot, flowerbed, fowlyard.
Fine earth in earth, they wait for resurrection.
Restored, unbreakable, they'll meet our lips
on some bright morning filled with lovingkindness.

GWEN HARWOOD

Bone Scan (Angus & Robertson, 1988); *Collected Poems 1943-1995* (University of Queensland Press, 2003); by permission of the Estate of Gwen Harwood.

■ Poetry Exhaustion is, I suspect, a more common phenomenon, than most poets will admit to.

Its symptoms are a general, hard-to-specify lack of concentration for and energy towards poems, including, and sometimes especially, those poets and poems which have previously seemed vital and essential. Personally speaking, I know if I pick up a book of Jaan Kaplinski, say, or Marie Howe, and find myself turning the pages without interest, I am surely in a period of Poetry Exhaustion.

Sometimes I bring this on myself. For reasons I do not fully understand I can, on occasion, be too ready to follow every whim of interest that I foster, reading up on poets that were previously unknown to me and buying their every book before breakfast, a process that, ten years ago, would have taken several trips to the library and to bookshops to set in motion.

Sometimes there is no reason for the exhaustion: it just happens. In these cases it is best to practise what Ken Smith once called 'absolute patience', for example by going to places where English is not spoken, or explicitly seeking out silence, until the poems begin to return. As a kind person once said to me: return to the last place you heard it speaking to you.

One of these places, for me, is Gwen Harwood's miraculous poem 'Cups'. Bookended in its first and final lines by mention of the 'lips' that they serve, the poem is a marvellous example of what can be achieved through the power of a single-minded concentration that merges religious language ('proverb', 'scripture', 'flocks', 'resurrection', 'restored') with the technique of personification, moving with apparent ease between the 'gregarious' and 'quietness'.

There is nothing in it I don't immediately say 'Yes!' to. As Seamus Heaney would say, it stays true to the facts of the matter, while lovingly doing nothing of the kind, inventing for these everyday artefacts the possibility of wisdom, holiness, marriage, death and even eternal life. That is quite an achievement for such a poem so transparently 'filled with lovingkindness'.

Avocados

I like the way they fit the palm –
their plump Buddha weight,
the sly squeeze for ripeness,
the clean slit of the knife,
the soft suck
as you twist the halves apart,
the thick skin peeling easily.
Naked, they're slippery as soap.

I serve them for myself
sliced and fanned
on white bone china
glistening with olive oil,
or I fill the smooth hollow
with sharp vinaigrette
scooping out
the pale, buttery flesh.

Every diet you've ever read
strictly forbids them.

ESTHER MORGAN
Beyond Calling Distance (Bloodaxe Books, 2001)

■ I heard Michael Symmons Roberts say at a reading once that poetry 'may well be marginalised, but it's still not going anywhere'. With its combined tone of obstinacy and realism, I like this remark very much.

When I find myself going in to bat with my non-poetry friends on such questions about poetry's efficacy in the modern world, those 99% of my acquaintances who look at me with affectionate, nervous sympathy, it is aphorisms such as these that I cling on to. Somewhere at the back of my kitbag I also try to remember to make space for poems such as Esther Morgan's 'Avocados'.

I came to it twice in quick succession in 2002, first in a magazine, then at a live reading at the Aldeburgh Poetry Festival. There are poems that you know you love and will always need well before you finish reading or hearing them. This is one of them. I think there is a good case to be made that poems as good as this are often apprehended as much by the body as the rational, conscious mind, on the nerve, as Frank O'Hara would say.

Partly this is down to its supple handling of successive alliterative-suggestive 'S' sounds: 'sly', 'squeeze', 'slit', 'soft', 'suck', 'skin', 'slippery', 'soap', 'serve', 'sliced', 'smooth', 'scooping', which find echoes in 'twist', 'ripeness', 'easily', 'myself' and 'glistening'. It isn't merely the appearance of the word 'naked' which prompts the forceful connection here between food and sex.

It is a miracle of a thing, bringing to mind the thing and activating desire of it in the same breath. Poetry will not go anywhere as long as poems like this continue to be written. Ask the avocado sellers at Aldeburgh.

June 30, 1974

(for Jane and Joe Hazan)

Let me tell you
that this weekend Sunday
morning in the country
fills my soul
with tranquil joy:
the dunes beyond
the pond beyond
the humps of bayberry –
my favorite shrub (today,
at least) – are
silent as a mountain
range: such a
subtle profile
against a sky that
goes from dawn
to blue. The roses
stir, the grapevine
at one end of the deck
shakes and turns
its youngest leaves
so they show pale
and flower-like.
A redwing blackbird
pecks at the grass;
another perches on a bush.
Another way, a millionaire's
white chateau turns
its flank to catch
the risen sun. No
other houses, except
this charming one,
alive with paintings,

plants and quiet.
I haven't said
a word. I like
to be alone
with friends. To get up
to this morning view
and eat poached eggs
and extra toast with
Tiptree Goosberry Preserve
(green) – and coffee,
milk, no sugar. Jane
said she heard
the freeze-dried kind
is healthier when
we went shopping
yesterday and she
and John bought
crude blue Persian plates.
How can coffee be
healthful? I mused
as sunny wind
streamed in the car
window driving home.
Home! How lucky to
have one, how arduous
to make this scene
of beauty for
your family and
friends. Friends!
How we must have
sounded, gossiping at
the dinner table
last night. Why, *that*
dinner table is
this breakfast table:
'The boy in trousers

is not the same boy
in no trousers,' who
said? Discontinuity
in all we see and are:
the same, yet change,
change, change. 'Inez,
it's good to see you.'
Here comes the cat, sedate,
that killed and brought
a goldfinch yesterday.
I'd like to go out
for a swim but
it's a little cool
for that. Enough to
sit here drinking coffee,
writing, watching the clear
day ripen (such
a rainy June we had)
while Jane and Joe
sleep in their room
and John in his. I
think I'll make more toast.

JAMES SCHUYLER
Collected Poems (Farrar, Straus and Giroux, 1993)

■ James Schuyler is probably best known for being a central member of the New York School of poets comprising Frank O'Hara, John Ashbery and Kenneth Koch. Having said that, it is probably fair to say that he is not as well-known as his compatriots, a state of affairs which is neither just nor entirely explicable.

I was reminded of Schuyler's delicate, unnerving, gossipy and immediate poems this week as I read an essay by my friend Cliff Yates in which he describes the composition of poetry as an act about itself as much as the 'subject-matter' at hand.

Schuyler's project can be categorised in this way, it seems me. His long poems 'The Morning of the Poem', 'A Few Days' and 'Hymn to Life' range widely in their content but are all ultimately about themselves as constructed annotations of minute lived experience. They do not pretend to have been written at one sitting, often notating changes in weather, seasons and news of friends and in the wider world; in this way they are catalogues of experience, more akin to albums of snapshots than portraits in close-up.

What makes Schuyler such a delight to read and re-read is that he was no less accomplished at the short lyric "poem of the moment". 'June 30, 1974' is a good example of how these poems often proceed: there are mentions of specific friends and places, gossip, tabletalk, and a rapturous adoration of the natural world. It is also a good example of the poem as enactment of its own composition.

I like spending time with Schuyler's poems very much. In contrast to his perhaps more famous colleagues I feel the need to read him very slowly, one poem at a time, savouring the experiences that are being described. I do think he was a great love poet, by which I mean he was in love with every second he was alive and with the process of writing it down.

His poem 'June 30, 1974' feels casual, almost throwaway. Can serious poetry be written at the kitchen table on a Sunday morning after a dinner party, while the rest of the house is asleep? Schuyler seems to imply not only that it can but that it is the true fountain spring of writing, among the dishes and the coffee cups, alone and in perfect quiet.

Prayer/Why I am Happy to be in the City this Spring

for creepers etched
        across a wall
        like the marble veins
        on *David's* hands;

for the lichen, moss
        and granite blocks
        of the city's ancient
        battlements;

for the empty paint pots,
        loose blue string
        and slightly sparkling
        bottled water
        discarded in the bushes,
        its dregs – quite still –
        reminding us
        we're only passing through;

for a builder's skip
        of silver crucifixes;

for sunlight on
        the golden rooster
        of a weathervane;

for a metal dragon
        listening
        to tingling cash
        outside the new café;

for students drinking coffee –
        their notes taking off
        in the wind;

for birdsong
    when a door slams;

for birch trees
    like Elizabethan ladies
    painted white;

for the burgeoning stems
    of *Aloe Vera*
    in municipal gardens
    like chubby children
    playing *Stuck-in-the-mud*;

for water in a concrete pond;

for reflections,
    fish
    and ripples
    over grey;

for buttercups emerging
    through drain holes;
    for garden planters
    standing bare all winter,
    now filled;

for distant hills;

for the balm of a snail's track
    on galvanised railings
    at midnight;

for this ongoing twilight
    over our new home
    and through it
    the relief of seeing
    individual stars.

ANDY BROWN
Goose Music (Salt, 2008)

■ I absolutely love this poem by Andy Brown. I am not sure when I read or heard it first. Possibly at one of Andy's readings in Exeter. Possibly in draft form at the writers' group we used to belong to.

To paraphrase what Kenneth Koch said on hearing Frank O'Hara's poems for the first time, there is nothing in it I do not like. Plus, I am a sucker for a good list poem.

There is so much pleasure in this poem. It makes me glad to be alive and to want to continue being so. I think I am secretly jealous of the line 'birch trees / like Elizabethan ladies / painted white'. I see pallid skin, fragility, the effort of keeping up appearances. Most of all it makes me see both objects in a fresh way. Brilliant.

It conjures for me perfect these liminal not-quite-here days of sunshine, warmth, sudden cold and increasing daylight.

There is nothing here which does not read completely freshly. Nothing that does not feel minutely observed, felt and processed from a core of complete respect for the world.

'Talk in another way'

The Picnic

It is the picnic with Ruth in the spring.
Ruth was third on my list of seven girls
But the first two were gone (Betty) or else
Has someone (Ellen has accepted Doug).
Indian Gully the last day of school;
Girls make the lunches for the boys too.
I wrote a note to Ruth in algebra class
Day before the test. She smiled, and nodded.
We left the cars and walked through the young corn
The shoots green as paint and the leaves like tongues
Trembling. Beyond the fence where we stood
Some wild strawberry flowered by an elm tree
And Jack-in-the-pulpit was olive ripe.
A blackbird fled as I crossed, and showed
A spot of gold or red under its quick wing.
I held the wire for Ruth and watched the whip
Of her long, striped skirt as she followed.
Three freckles blossomed on her thin, white back
Underneath the loop where the blouse buttoned.
We went for our lunch away from the rest,
Stretched in the new grass, our heads close
Over unknown things wrapped up in wax papers.
Ruth tried for the same, I forget what it was,
And our hands were together. She laughed,
And a breeze caught the edge of her little
Collar and the edge of her brown close hair
That touched my cheek. I turned my face in-
to the gentle fall. I saw how sweet it smelled.
She didn't move her head or take her hand.
I felt a soft caving in my stomach
As at the top of the highest slide,
When I had been a child, but was not afraid,
And did not know why my eyes moved with wet
As I brushed her cheek with my lips and brushed

Her lips with my own lips. She said to me
Jack, Jack, different than I had ever heard,
Because she wasn't calling me, I think,
Or telling me. She used my name to
Talk in another way I wanted to know.
She laughed again and then she took her hand;
I gave her what we both had touched – can't
Remember what it was, and we ate the lunch.
Afterward we walked in the small, cool creek
Our shoes off, her skirt hitched, and she smiling,
My pants rolled, and then we climbed up the high
Side of Indian Gully and looked
Where we had been, our hands together again.
It was then some bright thing came in my eyes,
Starting at the back of them and flowing
Suddenly through my head and down my arms
And stomach and my bare legs that seemed not
To stop in feet, not to feel the red earth
Of the Gully, as though we hung in a
Touch of birds. There was a word in my throat
With the feeling and I said, it's beautiful.
Yes, she said, and I felt the sound and word
In my hand join the sound and word in hers
As in one name said, or in one cupped hand.
We put back on our shoes and socks and we
Sat in the grass awhile, crosslegged, under
A blowing tree, not saying anything.
And Ruth played with shells she found in the creek,
As I watched. Her small wrist which was so sweet
To me turned by her breast and the shells dropped
Green, white, blue, easily into her lap,
Passing light through themselves. She gave the pale
Shells to me, and got up and touched her hips
With her light hands, and we walked down slowly
To play the school games with the others.

JOHN LOGAN

■ Mr Borton entered without speaking and with his back to us wrote at the top of the blackboard 'DO NOT REMOVE BOOKS FROM THIS ROOM', before turning round smiling and beginning the lesson.

All we had to do was read the poem in our *Touchstones* anthology and then talk about it, but it changed me completely.

The poem is a narrative of two adolescent children walking across fields one school lunchtime to eat their packed lunches 'away from the rest'. The poem evokes perfectly the 'soft caving in [the] stomach / As at the top of the highest slide' of giving and receiving a first kiss; and of the physical reactions to unexpected and barely articulated intimacy:

> There was a word in my throat
> with the feeling and I knew the first time
> what it meant and I said, it's beautiful.
> Yes, she said, and I felt the sound and word
> in my hand join the sound and word in hers
> as in one name said, or in one cupped hand.

While the poem did not describe experiences I had actually had, it conjured palpably a world with which I was entirely familiar: that of school, lunch hours, fields, streams, games and a vague but undeniably real sense of longing for something else, of not wanting to conform, perhaps.

You could say I connected with it.

Other important questions about this poem arose during the course of the lesson. One was to do with the poem's form, or what I would have then called the way it looked on the page. Oddly, the poem was laid out in one continuous stanza. Also, it did not rhyme, nor appear to have any regular rhythm. Indeed, if anything, it sounded more like someone talking. These were puzzling for several reasons. While the "poetry" I had experienced as a young child had largely been oral, I had not been made aware that printed poetry in books could attempt to replicate the rhythms of speech and appear to sound natural. On one level, therefore, the poem did not conform to my early expectations of what a poem could look or sound like at all: I felt it was more of a story than a poem.

On another level, however, I was more than intrigued because the poem was about experience I knew little about but was keen to discover. Furthermore, while I felt that the poem was 'like someone talking to me' I also knew that lines like those quoted above were not the way that people spoke. There was a sense that this was language which was both real and artificial at the same time.

I now identify these feelings as being to do with the interplay of concepts such as "form" with "content", or, "voice and feeling" with 'structure'. But at the time I felt a combination of intrigue and puzzlement. To borrow another phrase from the poem, I now see that the poem enacted 'talk in another way I wanted to know'.

Whenever I read or hear a poem I like for the first time I still feel that same caving as at the top of the highest slide. It is a kind of joyous nervousness. I want the poem to talk to me in a way I know and yet have no knowledge of. I am in the business of wanting to be surprised. I am already falling in love with the words taking shape in my throat and under my breath.

John Logan: *Ghosts of the Heart* (University of Chicago Press, 1960).

K563

As on most fine summer Sundays
we are breakfasting outside with our books.
This morning it is one of the Divertimenti
keeps the neighbours to themselves.
Now I can remember that man's name – Puchberg –
who funded Mozart when his wife was ill
        and the money coming in
wasn't covering the bills.
This is Vienna in 1788 in sunlight.

What are we supposed to do?
I open a conversation about Mozart
and you look up from the Penguin biography.
        The sky is a Prussian blue
and our back-yard garden is lit with music.

We are not yet thirty, and our lives
        are just about to start.
There is someone new, but that
is not why you are leaving. The cat,
who will be staying, stalks a daytime moth;
two stray poppies add a splash of colour.

It is very civilised. We are parting like friends.
On the breeze the churchbell tolls eleven.
Coming so far he won't arrive till three,
but your cases are already packed in case.
I've not slept properly for days
and now I need to be awake I find I'm dozing.
        When the record finishes
it is the hairfine crack in a teacup, ticking,
or a clock, perhaps, loud and very exact.

PETER SANSOM
Everything You've Heard is True (Carcanet Press, 1990)

■ I found Peter Sansom's poetry via a review by Ian McMillan in *Poetry Review*, in which he compared Peter's work with that of Alan Jenkins. In amongst talk of the *TLS*, the Northern School and *The North*, McMillan spoke with both delicacy and power of the sensibility at work in *Everything You've Heard is True*, Peter's debut collection for Carcanet. His point was that however slight the poems appeared, there was a much more subtle and restless spirit at work than the easy-going surfaces of the poems gave lie to.

A week or two later I found myself with a half-hour to spare in a bookshop, fell in love with the book's cover, and snapped it up on spec having read the poem 'K563'. At the time I did not understand the references to the music and life of Mozart (the title of the book is the tag-line used on the posters for the film *Amadeus*), but this did not put me off feeling compelled by the delicious feeling of witnessing scenes from my own life flash in front of my eyes.

The poem is about the end of an affair, but as I have returned to it over the years I increasingly think it both fits with and prefigures many of the themes in Peter's subsequent work: the place and "use" of art in everyday life, and the cost of making such artefacts (music, books, poems) in the lives of individuals and their families and loved ones. His third book, *Point of Sale*, is particularly interested in descriptions of 'the money coming in / [not] covering the bills', for example.

The poem's speaker appears not to have a choices: he can neither prevent himself from nodding off, nor the arrival of 'someone new'. The poem's energy is derived, it seems to me, from the tension set up by these descriptions which are in contrast with the choices the speaker is very explicitly active in presenting to us: 'the cat, / who will be staying, stalks a daytime moth'; the churchbells tolling exactly 'eleven'; the poppies' 'splash of colour'. The finish of the poem is indeed 'very civilised'. But what it seems to be doing, however, is questioning the work of the artist in noticing and articulating these details, as it were celebrating while cautioning its own artistry.

Words, Wide Night

Somewhere on the other side of this wide night
and the distance between us, I am thinking of you.
The room is turning slowly away from the moon.

This is pleasurable. Or shall I cross that out and say
it is sad? In one of the tenses I singing
an impossible song of desire that you cannot hear.

La lala la. See? I close my eyes and imagine
the dark hills I would have to cross
to reach you. For I am in love with you and this

is what it is like or what it is like in words.

CAROL ANN DUFFY
The Other Country (Anvil Press Poetry, 1990)

■ Like a lot of people I first came across Carol Ann Duffy's 'Words, Wide Night' as a Poems on the Underground poster. I can remember exactly where I was: on the Jubilee Line between St John's Wood and Finchley Road. I was travelling alone, and yes, it was night.

I was in that phase of trying to devour as much poetry as my time and income would allow. Finding this poem – and for free! – was a bit like the finger of God worming its way through the network of tunnels and affirming that decision.

In a tiny way, I felt like I had won the lottery.

Years later I would find an exact description for how it felt, late at night and exhausted, to discover I was no longer alone, in the words of Billy Collins's 'Marginalia': 'I cannot tell you / how vastly my loneliness was deepened, / how poignant and amplified the world before me seemed'.

But at that moment all I knew was gratitude to this plain-speaking ten-line poem of ordinary words. I felt it was in love with the 'pleasurable' 'singing' of words as I was, as much as and even more than the 'you' of the poem. This felt like the poem's true revelation and secret.

My hunch is that when poets meet the work of other poets, this is what they are looking for.

Atlas

There is a kind of love called maintenance,
Which stores the WD40 and knows when to use it;

Which checks the insurance, and doesn't forget
The milkman; which remembers to plant bulbs;

Which answers letters; which knows the way
The money goes; which deals with dentists

And Road Fund Tax and meeting trains,
And postcards to the lonely; which upholds

The permanently ricketty elaborate
Structures of living; which is Atlas.

And maintenance is the sensible side of love,
Which knows what time and weather are doing
To my brickwork; insulates my faulty wiring;
Laughs at my dryrotten jokes; remembers
My need for gloss and grouting; which keeps
My suspect edifice upright in air,
As Atlas did the sky.

U.A. FANTHORPE

New & Collected Poems (Enitharmon Press, 2010).

■ I heard 'Atlas' before I read it. I was in a tiny, tardis-like medieval church, at a rather posh wedding in Winchester.

Outside it was one of those perfect English summer days, clouds moving at walking pace, sweltering and benign. Yet tragedy stalked the minds of many of us involved in the service. A close family member of the wedding couple had recently died; the father of bride was seriously ill. Rumours of his inability to make it up the aisle abounded.

We were not to know it until the speeches in the marquee, but into this atmosphere of joy and reserve was to arrive one of the filthiest (and funniest) best man speeches any of us would ever hear…

To get there we had had to make arrangements. Relatives were persuaded to look after our children. A B&B was booked; outfits and presents were shopped for.

But I still think the main event of the day came half-way through the sermon in the wedding service itself. 'I hope you don't mind,' the vicar said, 'but I think this can best be expressed by reading you a poem' (what a wise man).

He was talking, of course, about love. One of the readings had been St Paul's hymn to the same in his letter to the Corinthian church. The poem he was now reading seemed much less familiar and twice as fresh. There seemed a clear-eyed, not at all romantic (or Romantic) appraisal of the facts of the matter. Some of the language (dry-rotten jokes?) seemed perilously close to cliché (which was precisely the point).

In a day that seemed to contain, as in so many English summer days, more than its fair share of tension and release, the poem appeared as unlooked-for balm and blessing. Most crucially it created a long moment in which all of the day's private sadness and public celebration could be held equidistant from each other, not so much for close examination but rather to allow acceptance to take a tentative foothold.

A moment of breathing, of infilled lungs, returning us to a larger moment, to each other and to ourselves.

The Lack of You

Level as any water, constant as clock-time,
The lack of you has occupied the house.
It is an unspent force, a static that fills
The space behind each closed and open door
With the same context. Now, all air contains
The closest memory and the most distant hope
Equally, cancelling neither, and still is empty.

And emptiest of all, the bed in which
We lay last night below the shield of the window,
Where past and future always round to become
Only what touch can tell – the curve of a nail,
The small of your back, the swell of smoothest skin
That falls away: where nothing now but moonlight
Drifts on the buoyant pillow, and time is endless.

LAWRENCE SAIL

Building into Air (Bloodaxe Books, 1995)

■ I first met Lawrence Sail at a private view at a gallery just outside Exeter. My family and I had just moved to the the city and our friends Rupert and Sue Loydell drove us out to the show so we could meet people.

The gallery, based in someone's house and perched on the edge of a precipitous Devonian hillside, had views across the valley which crackled in the late August heat. I felt as though we had swapped Brixton for Tuscany.

Having more of an eye on my children as they ran in and out of people's legs munching crisps than on the paintings, I think Lawrence and I must have exchanged the briefest of hellos before we moved on to other people.

Having got to know him since I know that even a five-minute chat with him in the street is always an education and a delight. We got to know each other mostly by bumping into each other at the shops. As my children grew up, there was no one who asked after them more solicitously or spoke to them with more openness than he.

I had heard Lawrence read many years before this, at a sponsored "poethon" event at the ICA to raise funds for the Arvon Foundation's Moniack Mhor writing centre. Each poet who read was asked to memorise ten minutes worth of their poetry, raising sponsorship from friends in the usual manner. I went with my parents. My father still speaks about Lawrence's magisterial 'Snooker Players'. He didn't fluff a line.

And now here he was asking my kids what they'd been up to recently.

Of all Lawrence's books, my favourite is his beautiful sequence of love poems in *Building into Air* (1995). The tenderness on display is absolutely within the English lyric tradition, framed around eternal polarities of separation/exhilaration, absence/fulfilment, which feels strikingly modern and direct. For my money it is one of the great sequences of love poems in English in the last twenty years.

The Birkdale Nightingale

(Bufo calamito – the Natterjack toad)

On Spring nights you can hear them
two miles away, calling their mates
to the breeding place, a wet slack in the dunes.
Lovers hiding nearby are surprised
by desperate music. One man searched all night
for a crashed spaceship.

For amphibians, they are terrible swimmers:
where it's tricky to get ashore, they drown.
By day they sleep in crevices under the boardwalk,
run like lizards from cover to cover
without the sense to leap when a gull snaps.
Yes, he can make himself fearsome,
inflating his lungs to double his size.
But cars on the coast road are not deterred.

She will lay a necklace of pearls in the reeds.
Next morning, a dog will run into the water and scatter them.
Or she'll spawn in a footprint filled with salt rain
that will dry to a crust in two days.

Still, when he calls her and climbs her
they are well designed. The nuptial pads on his thighs
velcro him to her back. She steadies beneath him.

The puddle brims with moonlight.
Everything leads to this.

JEAN SPRACKLAND
Tilt (Jonathan Cape, 2007)

■ I met Jean Sprackland in 2000, somewhere in the bowels of the Poetry Society in London. We were meeting to discuss a project we later called Poetryclass, a training programme for teachers wanting to make more of poetry in their practice. We shared some ideas, had a coffee and a good giggle, and have carried on like that, on and off, ever since.

I quickly learned that Jean is generous with her time and ideas and that she is kind. She is the best of teachers. And if you are reading this you will already know that she is an amazing poet.

Later that day I went up the London Eye for the first time. I connect the two events, corny as it may sound, because reading Jean's poems provokes in me that same feeling of giddiness, excitement and wonder at being shown the known world from completely unexpected angles.

As with most of my friends who are poets, I see Jean once a century. We gossip and natter, as you do. We will talk about who we are reading, which poets we are looking out for, that kind of thing. But we rarely speak about our own writing. (I have a very unscientific hunch that we are not alone in this.)

However, Jean did say two things to me about writing, a good while ago now, and I think they may permanently have changed me. Her first statement came as I was congratulating her for winning the Costa Poetry Award for her collection *Tilt*, saying how great it was, how layered and strange and evocative and how happy she must be to have her work recognised in this way. But she cut me off. 'It doesn't mean anything, not in the end, Anthony. All we ever have is the process.'

The other comment of Jean's I go back to and savour is this (made as an aside during a discussion about teaching the writing of poetry, I seem to remember): 'When I am writing I am only happy when I have no idea what I am doing.'

These have become touchstones for me. I use them to help me make judgements about how far I am committed to the process of writing the thing that is at hand, and how consciously controlling I am about the same.

I thought about these things driving home late on the motorway two weeks ago, as Jean's voice came out of the car radio, reading from her marvellous new book *Strands.* The passage we listened to concerned Jean's attempts to make a recording, under cover of darkness, of the extremely loud and distinctive mating call of the natterjack toad on the beach near Southport. Like talking to Jean it was life-affirming, full of deft touches of observation, and funny, in the best way possible.

Dusting the Phone

I am spending my time imagining the worst that could happen.
I know this is not a good idea, and that being in love, I could be
spending my time going over the best that has been happening.

The phone rings heralding some disaster. Sirens.
Or it doesn't ring which also means disaster. Sirens.
In which case, who would ring me to tell? Nobody knows.

The future is a long gloved hand. An empty cup.
A marriage. A full house. One night per week
in stranger's white sheets. Forget tomorrow,

You say, don't mention love. I try. It doesn't work.
I assault the postman for a letter. I look for flowers.
I go over and over our times together, re-read them.

This very second I am waiting on the phone.
Silver service. I polish it. I dress for it.
I'll give it extra in return for your call.

Infuriatingly, it sends me hoaxes, wrong numbers;
or worse, calls from boring people. Your voice
disappears into my lonely cotton sheets.

I am trapped in it. I can't move. I want you.
All the time. This is awful – only a photo.
Come on, damn you, ring me. Or else. What?

I don't know what.

JACKIE KAY

Darling: New & Selected Poems (Bloodaxe Books, 2007)

■ I first read 'Dusting the Phone' in a magazine. What struck me then and still strikes me now nearly twenty years later is the way the poem's title promises action but in fact describes very little actual 'dusting'.

I think it is a great example of the way the title of a poem can set up an expectation in the imagination of the reader, then explore the gap between what is promised and what is 'happening', which is the poem's real subject. In this sense the poem itself turns into a kind of 'hoax' while asserting itself as the voice of one 'trapped' between gratification and desire.

Reading it again I am struck by the poem's gentle and very subtle humour, the self-mocking dressing up and 'silver service' polishing; the playful absurdity of: 'In which case, who would ring to tell me? Nobody knows.' These are hints that the speaker is perhaps secretly relishing the pull and push tension of not being able 'to move', that not knowing what will happen when the phone once more fails to ring is perhaps the best place to be of all.

Rondeau Redouble

There is so little left. The room is bare.
She'll strip his sheets and blankets by and by –
only this morning he was sleeping there.
The light is pouring from a hard white sky.

She'll write to him, perhaps he will reply?
He's better off, she knows, God knows, elsewhere.
She'll be all right, she told him cheerfully.
There is so little left. The room is bare.

His smell's still hanging in the chilly air,
his motorcycle boots are propped awry,
helmet abandoned on the basket-chair.
She'll strip his sheets and blankets by and by.

Make a fresh start. Do something useful. Try
to avoid that stunned and slightly foolish stare
the mirror offers her maternal eye.
Only this morning he was sleeping there.

He's left a paperback face downwards where
he gave up reading and she lets it lie.
That's not his footstep coming up the stair.
The light is pouring from a hard white sky.

She stacks up papers, pulls the covers high,
faces the glass now, plucks the odd grey hair,
flicks away cobwebs, dusts off a dead fly,
feels and tries not to feel her own despair.
There is so little left.

DOROTHY NIMMO

The Wigbox: New and Selected Poems (Smith/Doorstop, 2000)

■ The back cover blurb of Dorothy Nimmo's *The Wigbox* sums up her personal and professional life in very few words: 'Dorothy Nimmo was an actress for ten years, a wife-and-mother for 25. In 1980 she started to write; in 1989 she ran away from home. She is currently caretaker of Settle Friends Meeting House.' *The Wigbox* was Nimmo's final collection. She died in 2001.

I am particularly struck by that line about running away. Isn't that what bored children do, of a Saturday afternoon, only to return half an hour later when they are hungry? Running away as an adult is a far more impetuous affair, foolhardy, even. It takes a rare kind of honesty to admit it. Something of the spirit of this lives on in her poems, which are by turns direct, matter of fact, nerveless, and heart-breaking.

If you don't know Dorothy Nimmo's poems, you have a treat in store for you. U.A. Fanthorpe was a fan, and A.S. Byatt. The latter, a friend from her time at Cambridge, had this to say about her poetry: 'They are sharp, black, dancing, profound and lyrical. They mix religious roots like Bunyan and George Fox with nursery-rhyme rhythms turned dangerous. They are tough and uncompromising – her world is bleak, and she records it with precise energy. It is also a world of difficult love, and the refusal of love, both mother-love, friendship and compassion. There is nothing quite like them.'

I encountered 'Rondeau Redouble' for the first time in the winter of 2006, at a gathering of poets and poet-educators at the Totleigh Barton writing centre in Devon. As I recall, Ann Gray gave the poem out at a workshop to near universal silence. A great poem of separation and loss, as well as a textbook handling of a given form, it seems to me, as Peter Sansom once said about Ciaran Carson, 'savagely controlled'.

It's the details of the poem that I love. The 'abandoned' motor-cycle helmet; the unfinished 'paperback face downwards'; the 'dead fly' which needs dusting off. Each of these works on a literal as well as figurative level, reinforcing the 'chilly air' of estrangement in the poem, which is itself reinforced by the repetition – and lived reminders – of stripped sheets and blankets. Cumulatively they intensify this atmosphere, earning the poem the right to name 'despair' as its real subject in the penultimate line.

Byatt is right, no one wrote like Dorothy Nimmo. If you will forgive the irony, she should be a household name.

Kin

'You make me sick!' this, with rancor, vehemence, disgust – again,
'You hear me? *Sick!*'
with rancor, vehemence, disgust again, with rage and bitterness,
arrogance and fury –
from a little black girl, ten or so, one evening in a convenience
market, to her sister,
two or three years younger, who's taking much too long picking
out her candy from the rack.
What next? Nothing next. Next the wretched history of the world.
The history of the heart.
The theory next that all we are are stories, handed down, that all
we are are parts of speech.
All that limits and defines us: our ancient natures, love and death
and terror and original sin.
And the weary breath, the weary going to and fro, the weary always
knowing what comes next.

C.K. WILLIAMS
Collected Poems (Bloodaxe Books, 2006)

■ In the spring of 1999 I got the best education in poetry I have ever had. I was in Suffolk, a guest of the Aldeburgh Poetry Festival for two weeks as poet in residence. The requirements of the residency were straightforward. I was to visit primary schools, colleges, prisons, libraries and local writers groups giving poetry writing workshops and readings.

It was the best of times. I got to meet and read with the great Connie Bensley; I got to try out ideas for teaching poetry with local teachers and schoolchildren; and I saw first-hand the triumph of dedication, hard work, inspiration and passion that goes into creating the special (and I would argue unique) culture of enthusiasm for poetry that is to be found on that part of the Suffolk coast.

For me the most formative aspect of this joyous time was the conversations I had in the car with my hosts Michael Laskey and Naomi Jaffa. In my experience there is always good banter, gossip and speculation to be had when poets meet and compare notes: who is reading whom, who is in form (or not), which are the new names to be looked out for etc. Joseph Brodsky called this 'the shopping list'.

What took this to another level in my experience at Aldeburgh was the intense close reading and enthusiasm that Michael and Naomi clearly brought to everyone they raved about. This is how I came to know C.K. Williams's 'Kin'.

Michael and I were on our way to a primary school in Sudbury. Stuck in traffic, but completely on time, we were nevertheless impatiently waiting at some lights outside a Spar shop when two young girls came out shouting at each other. Michael nudged me and said: 'It's just like that C.K. Williams poem, you know the one, where he says "the wretched history of the whole world". You know the one. You must do. There. It's there. In those girls. That poem.' I looked back at him blankly. I said I had read *A Dream of Mind* but did not know that poem.

'Come on, Anthony, you must. Bloody hell, what, you don't, I can't believe, it's there, right there, look!'

The girls had stopped walking and were now facing each other. The younger of the two was trying to reach the bag of crisps the older one was holding and eating from, tantalisingly out of reach of her sister. 'Do you know the poem? I can't remember what it's called now. Of course you do.' He quoted from it again: 'the wretched history of the world'.

At that the lights changed and we moved off.

As we got to the school I asked him for the name of the poem. By then of course the conversation had moved on. I had the distinct impression that there would be a sizeable chunk of homework waiting for me after the residency had finished. To paraphrase what Pound is supposed to have said to Eliot, I would have to modernise myself.

I'll never cease being grateful for that morning, and the ones I followed it. I sensed a burgeoning and a growth in my confidence first as a human and second as a writer in and through those tutorials with Michael and Naomi in their cars in the lanes of

Suffolk. It was and continues to be the best kind of education, one which pulses through me still each time I open *A Dream of Mind*, *The Singing*, and Williams's weighty *Collected Poems*.

The poem seems to me more prophetically powerful than ever, reaching far beyond my encounter with it through observing two young squabbling girls in a rural town on a February morning, and who, it now strikes me, will be old enough to have children of their own.

May the Silence Break

Because you do not speak
I know the shock
Of water encountering a rock.

Supremacy of silence is what I hate.
Only gods and graves have a right to that
Or one who knows what this is all about.

Perhaps you do.
If so, let something break through
The walls of silence surrounding you.

Out here among words
Your silence is like a magnet I am drawn towards.
Men's mouths, animals' eyes and the throats of birds

Fear this impenetrable thing.
So do I, all day long
And when the night drops like a confirmation

Of what you are,
Controller of every star,
Possessor

Of what the daylight struggled to reveal.
This possession kills
Whatever it wills.

Nothing I say matters tonight.
Nor should it.
This silence is right

Because it knows it is.
I shiver in the cocksure ice
And long for the warmth of bewildered eyes.

May the silence break
And melt into words that speak
Of pain and heartache

And the hurt that is hard to bear
In the world out here
Where love continues to fight with fear

And the war on silence will end in defeat
For every heart permitted to beat
In the air that hearts make sweet.

BRENDAN KENNELLY
Familiar Strangers: New & Selected Poems 1960-2004 (Bloodaxe Books, 2004)

■ I called this anthology *Lifesaving Poems* because I actually believe there is something redemptive and healing in the art of making, speaking, listening to and reading poems.

This may sound terribly old hat and beyond the pale, but I now feel I have lived long enough and seen enough things to have some kind of confidence, however tentative, in that claim. My first experience of seeing that working out in the life of someone else occurred in an encounter with 'May the Silence Break'.

Several years ago we got the news that a young family friend had been involved in a road traffic accident. She had been hit by a car whose driver had not stopped to attend to her. We found her in a hospital which specialised in head injuries. The doctors, in their frank way, said she would be affected for life by what had happened to her and while we could expect her to live she would need almost constant care.

The doctors encouraged us to speak to her, hearing being the most enduring of the senses. Would you mind if we read to her, we asked. They thought that was a good idea. Almost on a whim I took in Brendan Kennelly's *A Time for Voices* (Bloodaxe Books, 1990) to read to her. Partly this was because it was what I was reading at the time, but I also sensed that Kennelly was someone who knew about 'the war on silence' and the cost of trying to overcome it.

Plus, I felt I had nothing else to lose.

Over the next two weeks I read the poems to her, after work, as she slept.

Watching her now you would not know what had happened to her. She is married with children; she has a successful career. It is a miracle. Every time we speak I think back to those vigils by her bedside, watching the apparatus surrounding her help her breathe bleeping softly in the blue glow of the ward, praying for the silence to break.

The Switch

Someone loves the man who comes to my house
to lay wire. Someone loves the man who pours the concrete,
the one who tears up the shingles, the one who puts in
the studs. Someone loves the man who unrolls
the carpet. I know, because once

I kissed your smooth cheek in the morning
and watched you dress – denim shirt, jeans,
work boots, and a belt heavy with tools.
After you were gone I made coffee, made
the bed, made myself think of something – anything –
besides the heights where you worked, the hot wires
your fingers touched and how I loved those fingers,
the thick palms, the white crescents of your nails.

One day you threw a switch that almost killed you:
sparks, fire, burns that covered your hands and face.
It was before we met, but I saved the story,
took it out in the morning after you'd gone,
recited it like a rosary. I knew I could love you
into safety, pray your world right, smooth your life
like a bead between my fingers.

This morning I say the story again and wonder where you are,
which wires you are touching. Wonder who watches you dress,
who prays over your scars.

And wonder as I pour another cup of coffee just who loves
the man snaking wire from my attic to the basement.
I wonder who is praying for him as, right now,
he is throwing the switch.

LAURA APOL

Crossing the Ladder of the Sun (Michigan State University Press, 2004)

■ Laura Apol's 'The Switch' is a witty poem which explores the tension between primal, and sometimes unforeseen, forces and the surfaces of civilised behaviour.

The poem is "about" domestic electricity, both in terms of 'laying wire' and implicitly as having the kind of potency which can connect and divide people. We are in the territory of basic urges and dangers. I think the (surely not accidental) puns on 'laying' and 'studs' are risky in this regard, close to caricature. The 'switch' in the poem is also about more than supplying light to a room: partners and households are involved.

What the poem expresses in figurative terms it also achieves procedurally, switching back and forth between different narratives. This is witty, too, but it does not mask the poem's core question, the prayer, provoked by love, for protection from random injury. There is tension between the tenderness of the poem's tone ('I kissed your smooth cheek in the morning'; 'how I loved those fingers') and the implicit need for someone, somewhere, to 'pray [our] world right', 'smooth [our] life' and love us 'into safety'.

The culture we live in likes to argue that we are not in need of such security. Without the safety of easy guarantees or raising its voice, the poem persuades us that we are.

'What it's like to be alive'

What It's Like To Be Alive

(after Django Bates)

I remember the nights, and the sounds of the nights,
and the moon and the clouds, then the clear sky

and the stars and the angels on the Rye,
and I remember the way we knelt on the bed, how the bedclothes

were a tide, and the sunlight was a tide, and how everything pulled,
and I remember the trains, leaving and arriving,
and I remember the tears, your tears, and my tears

and how we were children, not lovers,
how the angels cried,

and I remember your face and you coming in my hands,
and the clouds, and the stars, and how, for a moment,
with our eyes tight closed how the planet lurched

and the angels smiled,
and I remember how I did not know if this was grief or love,

this hot pool,
and the sounds,
and then nothing.

A watermark held up to the light.
A boat rowed off the edge of the world.

DERYN REES-JONES
Signs Round a Dead Body (Seren, 1998)

■ Antony Dunn has a marvellous essay about his poetics, 'To Tell You the Truth', in *In Their Own Words: Contemporary Poets on Their Poetry* (Salt, 2012). There is a terrific line in the essay about having the ambition to write lines as good as those written by poets who inspired him to write in the first place. I like this. I think the social dimension of why we write poems, what Robert Pinsky calls a 'need to answer', seems to interest our culture less than those readily digestible aspects of poets' autobiographies such as their marriages and employment histories.

I am talking about what Raymond Carver calls real *influence*: that friendship or teacher or connection that sets your reading and interest off in a whole new direction because of a chance comment or recommendation. As Thomas Lux says in his digest of creativity theory, the great 'An Horatian Notion': 'You make the thing because you love the thing / and you love the thing because someone else loved it / enough to make you love it.'

We make some of these connections completely on our own, by reading the maze of influences we detect or read or hear about in writers we like. Others are thrust upon us as it were, with little choice in the matter, as when Rupert Loydell used to bollock me for not knowing about Mark Strand.

Rupert also had a hand in my first encounter with Deryn Rees-Jones's 'What It's Like To Be Alive'. He was editing the reviews page of *Orbis* at the time. I was mostly doing what I laughingly called freelance work, that is, earning not much money whilst looking after my children and doing the odd school gig or training with teachers. I'll come clean: to deepen what little social contract I had with poetry at the time, I kept my eyes on the free books Rupert would pass to me.

Of all the books I reviewed in this period *Signs Around a Dead Body* is the one I go back to. I still think it is a fantastic piece of work.

As when you first see or hear or read something you connect with but do not fully understand, part of my response to this book was 'How on earth did she do that?', quickly followed by 'I want to have a go!' If you do not possess a copy, you really need to get your hands on one right this second.

Mixed in with this awareness was the question, for me, of how far I would be prepared to ditch most of what I had thought was acceptable in a poem up to that point. I am not talking about the subject-matter of the poem here so much as its terms of direct address and urgent recall, its stark and repetitive vocabulary a child could understand. If I want to have a go at this, I thought, I am going to have to stop holding onto the same assumptions. It was as exciting as it was troubling.

Looking at the poem now I greatly admire how it is not ambitious for anything other than remaining within the cry of its eternal present moment. I comprises three sentences. One is long and multi-claused. The other two are short and declarative. When I first read them I thought of them as decoration, but increasingly I think they create a space in which their unambiguous finality not only lives and breathes but increases in mystery.

It is as though the speaker's linguistic synapses have been held in suspended animation for a moment of daydream and self-forgetfulness. They provide a vital pause, unglamorous in themselves but nevertheless taking the poem into a realm that is part grief and part elation. The sudden dip in temperature that they create is not unlike burying your hand below the surface of icy water. It is a most curious phenomenon, to read lines of such certainty sounding like the least certain utterances ever made.

Duty Psychiatrist

He nods, and looks serious.
Would you like to tell me
a bit more about that?

And she sighs, blurred and teary,
as she tells a bit more –
the bitter powder of the paracetamol,

the acid vomit, the pins and needles,
and the slipping away. And the bright
bringing back, charcoal and Parvolex.

EMILY RIALL
A Sinkful of Sky (Lulu, 2006)

■ Emily Riall will be a new name to most readers. She was a fine young poet beginning to find recognition for her work (*Foyle Young Poets of the Year 2002*, *Poems for Learning*, 2006) when she died suddenly in 2006. She was 22.

During the summer of that year I had the privilege of working with her on the manuscript of her first collection, *A Sinkful of Sky* (2006). I had seen various poems of hers before, but this was a revelation. We often talk approvingly about young writers who 'find their voice early', without actually saying what we mean by it. Emily's poems are a triumphant case study of that process in action.

First of all, she had found her subject. Most of what you will read in *A Sinkful of Sky* concerns the territory of mental illness. Without demeaning the seriousness of that topic, I would however say her real subject is the gaps between people, their silences and hesitations and the limiting effect of language on communication. Far from overwhelming her, she tackled these themes with great vigour and daring.

Secondly, Emily's poems are minor miracles of precision. There isn't a poem in her book which does not know when to stop. She seemed to have learned at a very early age that good poems trust their reader, providing them with information, yes, but also with space. Some writers can take years to learn this, but Emily apprehended it young, with laser-like self-knowledge.

This means the poems in *A Sinkful of Sky*, while full of personal biographical detail, nevertheless read like finished and achieved works of art. Direct in life and in her art, sometimes brutally so, it grieves me that she did not live to see her book published, nor to hear the praise it justly received. The deepest irony of all is that we will not see what Emily might have gone on to accomplish in her writing and her life, now indelibly fused in these amazing poems which preserve her memory with a force none of us could have predicted.

Twilight

Three minutes ago it was almost dark.
Now all the darkness is in the
leaves (there are no more
low garage roofs, etc.).

But the sky itself has become mauve.
Yet it is raining.
The trees rustle and tap with rain.
...Yet the sun is gone.
It would even be gone from the mountaintops
if there were mountains.

In cities this mauve sky
may be of man.

The taps listen, in the unlighted bathroom.

Perfume of light.

It is gone. It is all over:
until the hills close to behind
the ultimate straggler, it will
never
be so again.

The insect of thought retracts its claws;
it wilts.

MARGARET AVISON

The Essential Margaret Avison (The Porcupine's Quill, 2010)

■ I came across this poem one evening noodling on the internet when I had nothing better to do.

I was having one of my periodic bouts of Poetry Exhaustion. I was convinced I would never again come across a poem that would move me and that my entire library of poetry was worthless. I may even have persuaded myself that my twenty-five-year-plus dedication to poetry had been worthless and that a career change was in order, banking say.

As with many of these *Lifesaving Poems* I heard the poem before I read it, on this occasion via a YouTube clip of August Kleinzahler reading it at a prize-giving ceremony.

As I say, I was in the doldrums at the time, with no hope or expectation of anything resembling a poem ever coming into my life again.

Then bam, the tired, weary, slightly let's-get-to-the-bar-already voice of August Kleinzahler reading a poem about a Toronto Twilight by a woman I had never heard of, began to still my breathing. Then stop it altogether.

I am sure there was something about the combination of the tiredness I was feeling and the exhaustion in Kleinzahler's delivery that made me take notice. That, and the deceptively simple opening line: 'Three minutes ago it was almost dark.' Something about those short, declarative sentences, the way they innocently purport to paint a picture whilst carrying the weight of the world on their shoulders: 'But the sky itself has become mauve. / Yet it is raining. / The trees rustle and tap with rain.'

Something, also, in the way the poem carries commentary about the description of the scene it is describing: '(there are no more / low garage roofs, etc.).'; 'if there were mountains. // In cities this mauve sky / may be of man.'

Something of the way the poem turns hungrily towards metaphor, those taps listening in the bathroom, that 'Perfume of light.'

I felt the poem had no right to be playing with my expectations like this. How dare it offer commentary; how dare it mix outrageous, gorgeous metaphor with plain speech like that. How dare it not care what the reader thinks of it risking everything to tell us 'it is all over'.

Nevertheless, I succumbed to its 'insect of thought'. The poem still has it claws in me.

The Missing Poem

It would have been dark but not lugubrious. It would have been
fairly short but not slight. It would have contained a child
saying something inadvertently funny that was not said by my
daughter,
something strangely like what your daughter or sister said once
if you could remember. The child's voice flies across
a small parking lot where, in one of the cars,
a man and a woman sit listening to the silence between them.
The child's voice probably hurts them momentarily
with a sense of beauty apparently very possible
yet somehow out of reach. In the missing poem this is
implied, conveyed, transmitted without being flatly said.
And it does a dissolve into the look of a soccer field
after a game – the last three or four players walk
slowly away, their shin-guards muddy, their cleats caked,
one player dragging a net bag full of soccer balls –
the players seem to have known what it was all for
yet now they look somehow depleted and aimless there
at the field's far end; and a block away on a wood-grainy porch
the eyes of a thin woman sixty-three years old search the shadows
in each passing car, as the poem recalls what she wants to recall.
Hours later the field is dark

and the hills are dark and later even Firehouse Pizza has closed.
In the missing poem all this pools into a sense of how much
we must cherish life; the world will not do it for us.
This idea, though, in the missing poem is not smarmy.
Remember when you got the news of the accident –
or the illness – in the life of someone
more laced into your life than you might have thought;
the cool flash of what serious is. Well,
the missing poem brings that. Meanwhile not seeming like
an imitation of Mark Strand or Mark Doty or Mark Jarman!

Yet not like just another Halliday thing either.
Instead it would feel like a new dimension of the world,
the real world we imagine. With lightness!
With weight *and* lightness and, on the hypothetical radio,
that certain song you almost forgot to love.

MARK HALLIDAY
Jab (University of Chicago Press, 2002)

■ For first recommending Mark Halliday's work to me I remain indebted to Naomi Jaffa.

The blurb on the back of a recent pamphlet of his says this: 'Halliday isn't easy to categorise. Though described by poet David Graham as one of the 'ablest practitioners' of the 'ultra-talk poem' (a term coined by Halliday himself), ultra-talk is only one of the things he does. Intensely conscious of the presumption of the poet, he wriggles under his own critical microscope, wryly examining our 21st-century poetic stance. He is witty, wayward, sardonic and serious.'

This is a great summary of what Halliday is up to.

This poem comes in the final section of *Jab*, which contains just two poems, this one, the collection's closing poem, and 'Why Must We Write?' In a collection which is jammed to the gills with *tour de force* poems and tragicomic set-pieces these two poems seem to drop down to an even deeper level of seriousness and plaintive enquiry. It was a close-run thing which one I would choose for this anthology, and even now I find it hard to choose between them.

For one thing I love the amazing phrase-making that is on display here. Billy Collins has a line somewhere about good reading making him want to stand up and applaud from the bleachers – this is what Halliday does for me. I savour lines like 'their cleats caked', 'the field's far end', 'a sense of beauty apparently very possible' and 'listening to the silence between them'; I take them into my day and look for how they might become more real in my world; I weigh them; I hold them up to the light. I do not find them wanting.

On another level I do think that Halliday's point, in common with all good artists, can never be said too often: look at, love and 'cherish life; the world will not do it for us.' For me the turn in this poem occurs at the lines:

> Remember when you got the news of the accident –
> or the illness – in the life of someone
> more laced into your life than you might have thought;
> the cool flash of what serious is.

I remember reading that just after receiving the news of exactly that – a heart attack in the life of a friend of a friend, as you do. 'The cool flash of what serious is' is another great phrase which is equal to the suffering of the world and yet outstrips it at the same time. What Halliday does in this poem, it seems to me, is create an alternative universe in the shape of a mythical 'missing poem'. In reality, what is missing is not the poem, nor the world it portrays, but concentrated quality of attention to what stays right under our noses, day after day.

Looking at Them Asleep

When I come home late at night and go in to kiss them,
I see my girl with her arm curled around her head,
her mouth a little puffed, like one sated, but
slightly pouted like one who hasn't had enough,
her eyes so closed you would think they have rolled the
iris around to face the back of her head,
the eyeball marble-naked under that
thick satisfied desiring lid,
she lies on her back in abandon and sealed completion,
and the son in his room, oh the son he is sideways in his bed,
one knee up as if he is climbing
sharp stairs, up into the night,
and under his thin quivering eyelids you
know his eyes are wide open and
staring and glazed, the blue in them so
anxious and crystally in all this darkness, and his
mouth is open, he is breathing hard from the climb
and panting a bit, his brow is crumpled
and pale, his fine fingers curved,
his hand open, and in the center of each hand
the dry dirty boyish palm
resting like a cookie. I look at him in his
quest, the thin muscles of his arms
passionate and tense, I look at her with her
face like the face of a snake who has swallowed a deer,
content, content – and I know if I wake her she'll
smile and turn her face toward me though
half asleep and open her eyes and I
know if I wake him he'll jerk and say Don't and sit
up and stare about him in blue
unrecognition, oh my Lord how I

know these two. When love comes to me and says
What do you know, I say This girl, this boy.

SHARON OLDS

Selected Poems (Jonathan Cape, 2005), by permission of Penguin Random House UK

■ I found this poem in a collection of poems called *The Matter of This World* in a second-hand bookshop next to Berwick upon Tweed station. It was pretty much falling apart at the seams then, and has completley disintegrated now. I still have it. It may be one of my favourite books of all time.

The first British publication of poems by Sharon Olds – published in 1987 – it reminds me of a very particular time in my life, that of looking after and administering to the needs of my two young children. Parallel to this era, but not separated from it, was another kind of enterprise altogether, that of reading and writing as much poetry as possible.

I am not really sure if you can ever replicate the sheer hunger, obsession, desire and compulsion of your first serial encounters with poetry, at the point when you know you need it to breathe and make sense of who you are as much food and a roof over your head.

The closest thing I can compare it to is the love – animal, pre-verbal – that consumes you when you first have children. You tiptoe into their rooms at night, just to check that they are still breathing. Sometimes you wake them up, just in case. It is just like tinkering with a poem, getting up early or staying up late to delete just one more adjective, or comma, in case you get hit by a bus on your way to work the following morning only for the world to laugh at your incomplete and amateur work.

Nothing prepares you for it and nothing comes close to taking over your life in the same way again, not even illness or death. It is not a choice, finally, like falling in love. It is beyond that, existing somewhere in and outside of ourselves 'deep in unconsciousness' and 'anxious and crystally in all this darkness'.

A Letter to Peter Levi

Reading your poems I am aware
Of translucencies, of birds hovering
Over estuaries, of glass being spun for huge domes.
I remember a walk when you showed me
A tablet to Burton who took his own life.
You seem close to fragility yet have
A steel-like strength. You help junkies,
You understand their language,
You show them the stars and soothe them.
You take near-suicides and talk to them,
You are on the strong side of life, yet also the brittle,
I think of blown glass sometimes but reject the simile.
Yet about your demeanour there is something frail,
The strength is within, won from simple things
Like swimming and walking.
Your pale face is like an ikon, yet
Any moment, any hour, you break to exuberance,
And then it is our world which is fragile:
You toss it like a juggler.

ELIZABETH JENNINGS

The Collected Poems (Carcanet Press, 2012) by permission of David Higham Associates.

■ Some poets come into your life through the recommendations of friends, while others you find for yourself, in secret, without anyone else knowing.

Elizabeth Jennings falls into the second category for me. I have been trying to remember where and when I first read her, and I can't. My guess is I found her in an anthology – *The Oxford Book of Twentieth Century English Verse*, chosen by Philip Larkin. In that book you will find five perfect poems of hers: 'Delay', 'Song at the Beginning of Autumn', 'Answers', 'The Young Ones', and 'One Flesh', perhaps her best-known poem.

In any event, reading her by accident like this and hungry for more I devoured her short *Selected Poems*, published by Carcanet in 1979 as part of their Poetry Signature series.

'A Letter to Peter Levi' is not one of her famous poems, nor is it to be found in anthologies. It comes quite near the end of the original Selected, and is unusual in that collection for being comparatively informal in both tone and form.

I liked its conversational register straight away. Reading it is like coming across the proverbial letter of the title. We become complicit as readers in the poem's intimacy. I also liked it because it described a world which I knew nothing about and definitely wanted to know more of: knowing and being friends with other writers.

At the time I first read it I was unemployed and still living at my parents'. I found it remarkable that a simple thing like a walk taken by two writers where one shows the other a tablet in memory of another could be news, and moving.

Reading it again now I am struck by how often the poet uses the word 'yet' (four in total). I now see it as a masterful exercise in delayed gratification, the lift-off and magic of the last line coming after a long series of hesitations and qualifications and that amazingly offhand rejection of the poet's own simile of blown glass as strength and fragility. I had not seen this before, in any writing. I still think of it as an act of bravery, chutzpah and confidence.

Finally I think the poem is a great example of demythologising that most complicated of territories, the literary friendship. When Richard Ford wrote *Good Raymond*, his memoir of Raymond Carver, he said it was like writing about marriage: no one, least of all the protagonists, really knows the truth of what passes between two writers who are friends, rivals and equals. I like to think of this poem as coming closer than most attempts, built as it is on 'certain, solid thing[s]' ('Song at the Beginning of Autumn'), but not completely trusting of them either.

Literary Portrait

He can make fire
with his finger-ends

and into it go
letters he is sent
gifts he is given
people trees buildings

and in the curious
drifting smoke
he sings what he sees.

There is no one who sings
like him. Listen

but keep your distance.
He needs
a great deal of fuel.

EVANGELINE PATERSON
Lucifer at the Fair (Taxus, 1991)

■ I met Evangeline Paterson once, in the early 90s, at a workshop in London. Rupert Loydell suggested I went as we were both about to be published by *Stride*.

In the event it was more of a talk than a workshop. Evangeline's performance was a marvellous admixture of gossip, anecdote, and wisdom. She had an indomitable air, undercut by sudden vulnerability and charm.

The most memorable thing she said to us that day, prefaced by advice on the perils of poetry publishing in the small presses, was to ask us to pray for her writer's block. I found it extraordinary that a figure with her kind of track record and reputation would even have such a thing, let alone admit to it. She said it off the cuff, quite unannounced, as we were beginning to reach for our coats.

This unlooked-for utterance had a profound impact on me, not least in the way that I listen to poets when they speak about their work. How many of us abjure the vulnerability so wonderfully modelled by Evangeline that morning, preferring instead the easy answer about our writing process?

I think that same wry intelligence is present in her poem 'Literary Portrait'. It does not pull punches and settle for easy cynicism, even though its point is squarely made. It remains a lyric poem, not propaganda. In terms of form this is achieved in the reflective pauses at the end of each of its short lines. In terms of content, we are reminded again, in that stunning central stanza, of poetry as a 'curious/drifting smoke' and of the poet as one who 'sings what he sees'.

The toughness and the transcendence of this were also present in Evangeline. I dare to say I miss her.

Birth of the Foal

As May was opening the rosebuds,
elder and lilac beginning to bloom,
it was time for the mare to foal.
She'd rest herself, or hobble lazily

after the boy who sang as he led her
to pasture, wading through the meadowflowers.
They wandered back at dusk, bone-tired,
the moon perched on a blue shoulder of sky.

Then the mare lay down,
sweating and trembling, on her straw in the stable.
The drowsy, heavy-bellied cows
surrounded her, waiting, watching, snuffing.

Later, when even the hay slept
and the shaft of the Plough pointed south,
the foal was born. Hours the mare
spent licking the foal with its glue-blind eyes.

And the foal slept at her side,
a heap of feathers ripped from a bed.
Straw never spread as soft as this.
Milk or snow never slept like a foal.

Dawn bounced up in a bright red hat,
waved at the world and skipped away.
Up staggered the foal
its hooves were jelly-knots of foam.

Then day sniffed with its blue nose
through the open stable window, and found them –
the foal nuzzling its mother,
velvet fumbling for her milk.

Then all the trees were talking at once,
chickens scrabbled in the yard,
like golden flowers
envy withered the last stars.

FERENC JUHÁSZ

translated from the Hungarian by David Wevill

Sándor Weöres and Ferenc Juhász: Selected Poems, tr. Edwin Morgan & David Wevill (Penguin Books, 1970)

■ Mark Halliday has a hilarious essay which dissects his teaching of poetry called 'Moose Failure'. What 'The Moose' is to Halliday, 'Birth of the Foal' means to me. I love it with a passion, to the extent that I feel I'd give my arm to write lines like:

> And the foal slept at her side,
> a heap of feathers ripped from a bed.
> Straw never spread as soft as this.
> Milk or snow never slept like a foal.

But there are other, less kind, parallels. Friends, I murdered this poem in the classroom. Let's call it Foal Failure.

A bit of background. To generate data for my doctoral study of teaching poetry writing with primary-aged schoolchildren I taught a two-hour class of 30 nine- and ten-year-old children once a week for two years. We read, performed, analysed, cut up, talked about, argued over and wrote poems each week, with varying degrees of success and joy and comfort.

Even though I did not really know what I was doing I think it was one of the happiest times in my life. I am still learning from it now.

Of all the poems we looked at, the gap between my expectations – based on my deep love of the poem concerned – and what actually occurred, was probably greatest with 'Birth of the Foal'. And not for one minute do I blame this on the children.

I wanted them to love it as much as I did, so ran lessons on it for three consecutive weeks. It was spring; the poem was about spring. They loved animals; the poem was about animals. They had been studying life-cycles; the poem was about life-cycles. What was not to love? What could possibly go wrong?

By the end of this time I think I had pretty much undone all the goodwill towards poetry that I had painstakingly built up during the previous year. If I had listened I would have seen that the children struggled with the poem almost from the word go. I would have seen that the intensely metaphorical gaze of the poem was beyond the capacity of those children at that time to sustain meaningful engagement with. I would have seen that they had started to behave disruptively. Like a fool, I pressed on. For six hours, over three weeks. I would have seen that they hated it. And me.

Foal Failure.

If any of them are out there reading this (I guess they'd be in their mid-20s by now) I'd like to say sorry. But I'd also hope they might give the poem just one more chance. I'd like to think it still might get them all 'talking at once', with or without their envy withering 'the last stars'.

Results

Of course it was always going to be secret,
an envelope no one would know had arrived
that I'd lock myself in the bathroom to read.

Nothing like coming down late to breakfast
and you saying 'How you failed history
I'll never know.' Or standing in a queue

in the only taverna with a land line,
the owner grinning between black teeth
while I ask you 'How did it go?' and wait

for a pause that might mean well, or not.
Out on the terrace the old dog gets up
and drags his chain two steps into the shade.

SIÂN HUGHES
The Missing (Salt Publishing, 2009)

■ I first encountered Siân Hughes's poems sitting around a table with some talented teenage poets at the Arvon Foundation's writing centre at Lumb Bank. We were looking at her poem 'Bear-Awareness and Self-Defence Classes' (subtitled 'Or Fathers and Husbands'). Like many of Siân's poems it is short and made of words and sentences an eight-year-old could read. But while its subject-matter is about what happens to some children, it is absolutely not a poem for all children.

I will be honest, as I listened to the discussion of Siân's poem I did wonder if I was missing something. I wondered if the poem was all it was cracked up to be, these plain words arranged over three ordinary quatrains, which suddenly just stop.

And then it hit me. Like being winded. Like waking up in a sweat. Like the air leaving the room.

The point of this poem about domestic violence (as I read it) is the control with which it is executed, through the simple-looking but deadly metaphor of wild bears. Painful subject-matter has been rendered truthfully and (apparently) artlessly, with no poetical high flourish and certainly no moralising. The unstated words of comfort implicit in the poem iterate in nothing more than a whisper that by being truthful, by using song to describe our suffering we can overcome what threatens to overcome us.

Siân Hughes does this in poem after poem in her book *The Missing* (2009). I nearly wrote 'pulls off this trick' in that last sentence. The reason I did not is because I do not think what is going on here is about literary artifice alone. I think it is a genuinely held moral position of the writer that she chooses tact and taste over coshing her reader with Misery. Choosing to make the poems appear slight is, therefore, one of risking being branded inconsequential, when they are anything but. In this way I think the poems share some similarity with the work of Hugo Williams.

As I read it, this poem is about three sets of results: those being read about in a locked bathroom, those concerning a failed exam, and those being relayed over a bad phone line. By concentrating on the latter, the poem craftily moves our attention away from the main action, which is in the bathroom with the envelope. The clue to these results being the poem's authentic subject is contained in the words 'Of course' and 'always', with their sense of prefiguring the inevitable.

What is actually described, though, is a queue, a waiter, a silence, and a dog. I love the owner's black teeth. He has a two-second cameo in Siân's book and yet I will know him forever. (Siân would make a fine film director, perhaps.) I love the placing of the word 'wait' at the end not just of a line, but of a stanza, emphasising the ensuing pause, the articulate gap between words we all know but would rather avoid. And most of all I love the dog.

I love the comforting-sounding chiming of two doom-laden words: 'chain' and 'shade'. I love the undercutting of this comfort which the words 'dog' and 'drags' perform, their bare bones d's and g's contrasting with the 'ch' in 'chain' and the 'sh' in 'shade'. We are not told any more about the envelope in the bathroom because we do not need to be.

Some of the Usual

Standing in the kitchen before breakfast, not including some of
the usual –

what to buy in Budgens now your Melitta coffee's been discontinued
how the *Today* programme's become so tabloid
how rarely we make love
what thirteen new houses going up bang next door will do to the
village
not having children
whether I should read *British Dressage* or *Poetry* on the loo
those knife attacks on pregnant mares
the rat I'm watching eating our bird seed
the rust I can't yet see on the Honda
the chances of ever having jutting hipbones and a flat stomach again
the arrival of occasional hairs on my nipples and chin
why I like most men to want me (even though I don't want most
men)
whether the climate's really fucked
long-term immune system damage from additives
how many Camel you smoke
lack of religious faith
my waking up one morning and you not
cervical cancer
never having had children
ever having to nurse my mother
the day when I won't be able to telephone her anymore
female circumcision
what the Taliban have done to women
whether deep down I prefer women to men
why I'm so elaborately nice to people I can't stand
irreparable hard drive corruption (with no files backed up)
keeping white geraniums frost-free with nowhere to store them
always missing the last overseas posting date for Christmas
last summer's wasps hibernating in the loft

– before breakfast and since last night, I've mostly been worrying
about getting it wrong:
that perhaps *American Beauty* may not after all be a film of heart-
breaking, staggering genius.

NAOMI JAFFA

The Last Hour of Sleep (Five Leaves Publications, 2003), by permission of the author

■ The first thing I do when a new copy of *The North* or *The Rialto* lands on the doormat is to see if there are any of my friends in it. I know I am not alone in walking around with what I think of as "my team" (poets I know and have worked with; poets I have not met but whose work I adore) looking over my shoulder at what I do. I use this as an excuse to fire off encouraging emails to them straight away with things like 'Great poem' in the subject line. What do you mean, you do not do this too?

As I have said before, all we really have as poets is the process, but this does not stop me relishing giving and receiving support from those whose work I admire.

I first came across Naomi Jaffa's 'Some of the Usual' in *The North*, and was delighted when she opened her terrific pamphlet of poems *The Last Hour of Sleep* with the same.

'Some of the Usual' is a great list of weariness and anxiety that somehow manages to sound joyful and celebratory. There are many references in it to violence, death and disease; the horror of ageing – of the speaker and those the speaker loves – stalks every line, it seems.

For the record I think it reads as powerfully and prophetically as it did when Five Leaves brought it out in 2003, which is to say that references to the Taliban, female circumcision and climate change remain as current and pressing as ever.

The world the poem inhabits and recreates is both global and domestic, therefore. The line between a rat on the bird feeder and global warming is deliberately blurred. The poem succeeds in outstripping these events and persuading the reader they are all somehow vital and of a piece because of its great consistency of tone, which comes across as almost casual, spoken, concerned and self-aware all at once.

The poem builds a kind of force-field of rapt inclusivity: detail after detail is presented apparently bare-handedly but with such precise attention to the process of their presentation as to make them quietly extraordinary. Notice the force of 'why I like most men to want me' compared to the easier to write 'why I want most men to like me', for example.

Finally, I think 'Some of the Usual' pulls off that rare trick in poetry, of delivering a punchline that is both memorable and worthy of the poem it serves. This is in no small part due to the skilful handling of the voice – direct, engaged, a little bit frayed at the edges – in the lines which precede it. For the record, I am with Naomi on this: if you want a film which really goes under the fingernails, watch *The Ice Storm* instead. She is also right about the *Today* programme which grows more *Daily Mail* by the day.

Morning

The gentleness of secretaries in the morning is something
to behold. When they are arriving, fluttering through the
office and settling to their desks. They are cheery when
exchanging greetings and stories. I have noticed the
gentleness of secretaries before the day sets in and
before they are no longer available to themselves.

CAROLINE YASUNAGA
Hard Lines 3 (Faber & Faber, 1987)

■ 'Morning' seems to me a marvellous example of unadorned simplicity, both tonally consistent on its own terms and entirely suited to its occasion.

Ann Sansom has a great workshop exercise involving writing about mornings using the poems of Billy Collins and Jonathan Swift. I think Caroline Yasunaga's poem is up there with them. It is the only poem of hers I have seen.

This is a shame, because 'Morning' is perfect.

It is a poem of presence and paying attention. In drawing attention to its own noticing, of 'gentleness', 'greetings' and 'fluttering', the poem requires us to observe what is otherwise forgotten before 'the day sets in', transforming its occasion as it proceeds, but never seeking to outstrip it. I can't ask for more.

I Would Like to be a Dot in a Painting by Miró

I would like to be a dot in a painting by Miró.

Barely distinguishable from other dots,
it's true, but quite uniquely placed.
And from my dark centre

I'd survey the beauty of the linescape
and wonder – would it be worthwhile
to roll myself towards the lemon stripe,

Centrally poised, and push my curves
against its edge, to get myself
a little extra attention?

But it's fine where I am.
I'll never make out what's going on
around me, and that's the joy of it.

The fact that I'm not a perfect circle
makes me more interesting in this world.
People will stare forever –

Even the most unemotional get excited.
So here I am, on the edge of animation,
a dream, a dance, a fantastic construction,

A child's adventure.
And nothing in this tawny sky
can get too close, or move too far away.

MONIZA ALVI

Split World: Poems 1990-2005 (Bloodaxe Books, 2008)

■ I first read Moniza Alvi's wonderful 'I Would Like to be a Dot in a Painting by Miró' in the book she shared with Peter Daniels, *Peacock Luggage* (Smith/Doorstop, 1992). The selection of poems she chose to publish in this book also appeared in *The Country at My Shoulder*, her debut full-length collection with Oxford University Press, not long afterwards.

The feeling I had on finishing reading the poem was something close to elation, I remember. I felt transported to a completely different world and way of looking at the same, by a voice that sounded completely self-assured. Here was someone, I thought, who had arrived.

On the surface the poem is not self-consciously "about" the poet at all. Choosing to speak in an assumed voice about the overlooked 'dot', it nevertheless tackles huge subjects: of art, gender, race and sexuality at the margins. This is all done in a voice which sounds effortless, chatty even. It is also explicitly a poem of 'joy' and celebration.

I have read the poem countless times over the years and the more I do so, the more I think that its most important line is not the description of the 'tawny sky', the 'lemon stripe' or the 'beauty of the linescape', gorgeous though those phrases are. The more I read this poem the line that cuts me in two each time I do so is its unassuming centre: 'But it's fine where I am.'

At first reading I thought this comically throwaway, and not terribly poetic to boot. What I have come to appreciate about it over the years is the way it lends the whole piece a tone of lightness. Without it the poem struggles to achieve its concluding note of acceptance, of relish in imperfection. The poem holds in tension the reality of life at the 'edge', a space it denotes as 'fine'. This is the 'adventure' at the heart of the poem, it seems to me, which, for all its lightness of touch, is a deadly serious challenge.

Women Who Dye Their Hair

Some of us have done it since our twenties
when our hair turned white on the death of a loved one
or it ran in the family like baldness, and some of us
spray red or purple on shaved stubble,
and others have let it creep up on us,
countnig the odd hair, then the fifth, the fiftieth,
till our teenagers point out how old we're getting
but our lovers who hate anything artificial
like make-up and sequins, though they accept
icecream and the Pill, say we shouldn't bother,
so we steal home from Boots with the ColorGlo
and lock ourselves in the bathroom in rubber gloves,
emerge an hour later ten years younger
with a smart grey streak over one temple
and mahogany smudges round the jaw line.
And when the roots start to show we carelessly
pop into the hairdresser and book a colour
which means a cut and finish and takes all morning
so we can catch up on our reading, extending
our knowledge of the stars and multiple orgasm,
but we have to go every six weeks or it starts to fade
and by now the local firm is turning our hair to hay
so we find a better one at fifty quid a splash,
a rollercoaster we can't get off of,
and we decide to let it all grow out and be our age
which isn't a hundred and five but might as well be.

JANET FISHER

Women Who Dye Their Hair (Smith/Doorstop, 2001)

■ I first had the pleasure of reading this remarkable and delightful poem by Janet Fisher in 2001 in the company of a room full of chuckling people with Ann Sansom at the Arvon Foundation Writing Centre at Totleigh Barton. It is from her wonderful collection of the same name.

What I felt about the poem then, and still feel now, is that it appears artless, almost 'careless', as the poem has it. It is anything but. Comprising just two sentences, it is a bravado display of control which moves between defiance and despair, so neatly encapsulated in the final line.

It is a brilliant example of how a poem can appear to be "about" one thing (dyeing your hair, secret trips to Boots), but is just as much "about" other things (age, sex and death). The tension between the 'artificial' products described and the inevitability of being told you look old by teenagers is what gives the poem its energy and 'finish'.

If you haven't read Janet Fisher's work before, this is a great place to start – but you should also check out her wonderful book *Brittle Bones* (Salt, 2008). I do think she is one of the sanest poets who has ever lived.

‘I came near to dying’

Alone

I

One evening in February I came near to dying here.
The car skidded sideways on the ice, out
on the wrong side of the road. The approaching cars –
their lights – closed in.

My name, my girls, my job
broke free and were left silently behind
further and further away. I was anonymous
like a boy in a playground surrounded by enemies.

The approaching traffic had huge lights.
They shone on me while I pulled at the wheel
in a transparent terror that floated like egg white.
The seconds grew – there was space in them –
they grew as big as hospital buildings.

You could almost pause
and breathe out for a while
before being crushed.

Then something caught: a helping grain of sand
or a wonderful gust of wind. The car broke free
and scuttled smartly right over the road.
A post shot up and cracked – a sharp clang – it
flew away in the darkness.

Then – stillness. I sat back in my seat-belt
and saw someone coming through the whirling snow
to see what had become of me.

II

I have been walking for a long time

on the frozen Östergötland fields.
I have not seen a single person.

In other parts of the world
there are people who are born, live and die
in a perpetual crowd.

To be always visible – to live
in a swarm of eyes –
a special expression must develop.
Face coated with clay.

The murmuring rises and falls
while they divide up among themselves
the sky, the shadows, the sand grains.

I must be alone
ten minutes in the morning
and ten minutes in the evening.
– Without a programme.

Everyone is queuing at everyone's door.

Many.

One.

TOMAS TRANSTRÖMER
translated from the Swedish by Robin Fulton
New Collected Poems, tr. Robin Fulton (Bloodaxe Books, 2011)

■ I was drawn to this poem by Tomas Tranströmer long before the opening line 'One evening in February I came near to dying here' took on a special resonance when I was diagnosed with Non-Hodgkin's Lymphoma on Valentine's Day, 2006. On first reading it reminded me of the time that our family car similarly skidded sideways on ice in the Jura mountains after we had spent Christmas with my mother's family.

I especially liked the description of slow-motion panic and frustration: the 'transparent terror that floated like egg white. / The seconds grew – there was space in them – / they grew as big as hospital buildings.' I like the risk in these images, the connecting of the familiar and everyday to an abstract and real state of terror. But describing time as big is not especially new, maybe even clichéd; and the poet risks overstating his case by linking this idea with what is perhaps obvious in the case of a car accident: hospital buildings. The effect is both immediate and otherworldly, apprehended as though pre-verbally in these highly cinematic images.

The second part of this poem describes the effect of this incident in the life of the poem's speaker: 'I must be alone / ten minutes in the morning / and ten minutes in the evening. / – Without a programme.' It is as though the events described in Part 1 of the poem take the speaker into a space in which only silence can provide succour and reassurance in a world where 'Everyone is queuing at everyone's door.'

There is a quiet determination in these lines, yet they do not attempt to offer an overt reassurance of their own. Tranströmer presents, he does not preach. In their take-it-or-leave-it finality the closing lines of this poem similarly guide the reader into a new contemplation of space and silence, advocating them neither as threatening nor essential.

With Only One Life

Hold with both hands
The tray of every day
And pass in turn
Along this counter.

There is enough sun
For everybody.
There is enough sky,
And there is moon enough.

The earth gives off the smell
Of luck, of happiness, of glory,
Which tickles your nostrils
Temptingly.

So don't be miserly,
Live after your own heart.
The prices are derisory.

For instance, with only one life
You can acquire
The most beautiful woman,
Plus a biscuit.

MARIN SORESCU
translated from the Romanian by D.J. Enright with Ioana Russell-Gebbett
The Biggest Egg in the World (Bloodaxe Books, 1987)

■ I heard 'With Only One Life' before I read it. It was one of the first poetry readings I had been to, a 24-hour sponsored 'poethon' at the ICA to raise funds for the then decrepit Moniack Mhor writing centre in Scotland.

The idea was that each participating poet had to recite from memory ten minutes of their poetry to qualify for sponsorship by friends and family, in the usual manner. (I can still remember who cheated by whipping out copies of their books.)

Marin Sorescu, whose English was non-existent, was accompanied by Alan Jenkins offering a line-by-line translation 'for those of us whose Romanian [was] a bit rusty'. As I remember, it was the highlight of the evening, poem after wry poem delivered in declamatory Romanian, each line pursued by its after-echo in impeccable English.

It could be rose-tinted spectacles, but I clearly remember the audience falling around laughing at the final line of 'With Only One Life'. I still love its underlying seriousness, almost in spite of its utterly clear translation and plain-speaking tone.

Deep Third Man

(Poem for a retired wicket-keeper)

That leg-side stumping of yours
hangs safe in the memory
(if not of the man you stumped).

But then you said that the bowler
who started the incident off
was a medium-paced

maths teacher, who would never
leap to conclusions nearly
as quick as yours,

but kept to a length, I guess,
and showed his workings, how he got
wherever he got,

then went to deep third man.

HUBERT MOORE
The Hearing Room (Shoestring Press, 2006)

■ I came across Hubert Moore's fantastic book of poems *The Hearing Room* via Lawrence Sail.

In the autumn of 2006, in the period between the end of my chemo and radiotherapy treatments for cancer and my return to work, I used to go round to Lawrence's house for coffee once a week where we would sit and mull on whatever came into mind: poetry, art, writing, childhood and of course, the body. It was the best kind of conversation and healing: unprogrammatic, non-linear, sometimes with false starts, but shot through with generosity and nurture.

Looking back at our chats from this distance I imagine Lawrence must have thought I had shell-shock. On more than one occasion I would try to reply to him only to trail off into bizarre non-sequiturs or silence…

As always with Lawrence there was learning (and for free!) in the shape of quotes and anecdotes from the amazing library of his mind. There were also book recommendations, hundreds of them. I should have kept a notebook, but to my shame I did not. (In my defence I was in no state to write anything down.)

But Lawrence did keep mentioning one writer in particular, someone whose work I did not know. 'You must read Hubert Moore. He's a fantastic poet and no one's heard of him. He's written this marvellous book of poems all about being at deep third man.'

Poetry Exhaustion is not a welcome state of mind in the life of any poet. Sometimes it is self-inflicted. Sometimes the causes come from outside, as I was experiencing right then in my grief-shock.

But something Lawrence said, and the way he said, it caused a tremor of interest in the numb recesses of my mind. Perhaps he knew I was a sucker for cricket-related literature. Perhaps it was his mention of Hubert Moore's interest in working with victims of torture. To make sure he would know I understood him, and because he is unfailingly generous, he gave me the book for Christmas.

If you do not own *The Hearing Room* you really do need to get hold of a copy. There are poems which relay the voices and experiences of those who have been tortured; and there are poems (three of them: yes!) about being at deep third man. But really the book is a hymn to humanity and to love. It is a book of grief and silence. On each page there is a profound sense of how far words will take you, and how far they will not. To call it beautiful is to make it sound pretty, because much of it is not. It is a seriously beautiful book.

Like the next poem, it is "about" infinitely more than it seems to be "about".

So Lawrence handed me this book at Christmas 2006. As the days began to grow lighter I began reading it. To borrow from the title of one of Lawrence's own books, I began to feel poetry and the world returning to me.

The Beautiful Apartments

The thought working its way towards the light.
LUDWIG WITTGENSTEIN, 1946

In the empty block
across the lake from here
you notice first a light
go on go off go on again.

You wonder who
at this late hour
stirs in rooms
darkness uninhabits.

And then yourself, alone,
gazing from a room
towards the light
across the lake from here.

GEORGE MESSO

■ I first read 'The Beautiful Apartments' when I was given *Entrances* as a birthday present the year after I was told I was in remission from non-Hodgkin's Lymphoma. This is important because while I was glad to be alive and celebrating with friends, deep down I was not in the best of spirits. I felt the winged and sacred thing of poetry had left me. Not in terms of writing (I was kind of ready for that), but in terms of reading.

You see, reading, not writing, is what it is all about. I once heard Stephen Knight say the only way he knows he is writing well is when he is reading well.

And I was reading nothing.

Our guests were coming through the door, coats were being taken off and drinks poured. I was handed a very slim parcel with my name on it. I confess I had never heard of George Messo. But committing to the moment I opened the book at random (what I always do with any book of poems) and began reading where my eye fell.

'The Beautiful Apartments' is the poem I read. I credit it with re-engaging me in the world of poetry after my period of Poetry Exhaustion. It is beautiful, simple and strange, all at once. A ten-year-old could read it. On reading it I felt I was finding my bearings again, like finding faith, the phone number of an old friend, or a light switch in a darkened room, which once illuminated seemed more familiar than before, as if previously seen in a dream.

Chemotherapy

I did not imagine being bald
at forty-four. I didn't have a plan.
Perhaps a scar or two from growing old,
hot flushes. I'd sit fluttering a fan.

But I am bald, and hardly ever walk
by day, I'm the invalid of these rooms,
stirring soups, awake in the half dark,
not answering the phone when it rings.

I never thought that life could get this small,
that I would care so much about a cup,
the taste of tea, the texture of a shawl,
and whether or not I should get up.

I'm not unhappy. I have learnt to drift
and sip. The smallest things are gifts.

JULIA DARLING

Sudden Collapses in Public Places (Arc Publications, 2003)

■ I was astonished to find in an old diary that by 8 March 2006, less than one month after I was diagnosed with cancer, I had already been given two infusions of chemotherapy. The speed of the cycles of my particular treatment was due to my successful volunteering to take part in a randomised control trial testing the efficacy of a cycle of 14 days against 21 days, or, in the jargon, 'CHOP-R 14 vs 21'.

It is odd what you remember. The twenty tiny cherry-red pills I had to swallow with milk during for five days after each infusion. (These were steroids. They were deeply un-fun, let me tell you.) The Piriton chaser injection just ahead of the main infusion, 'to send you away with the fairies, my lover', as one nurse put it. She wasn't wrong.

Most of all I remember the swathes of bright blue clothing every nurse had to wrap themselves in each time they began the course of injections. When I asked why this was necessary I was told it was because the chemicals were so poisonous they would burn through ordinary clothing if spilt. 'And to clean it up we would have to shut the whole ward down. For a day.'

Mostly I looked forward to being away with the fairies.

I had come across Julia Darling's marvellous poem 'Chemotherapy' nearly a year before I fully understood what she was talking about. There is not much I need to add to it, except to say I think 'the smallest things are gifts' sums up for me the entire universe of pain, gratitude, suffering, relief, anxiety and humour which the word 'cancer' registers in me.

■ I did not come across Psalm 102 ('A prayer of an afflicted man. When he is faint and pours out his lament before the Lord') until some after my treatment had ended. Again, I do not think it needs much explication. My first reaction to it was – how did the psalmist know how to describe the bodily reaction to chemotherapy thousands of years before it was invented?

Psalm 102

(verses 1–7)

Hear my prayer, O Lord;
  let my cry for help come to you.
Do not hide your face from me
  when I am in distress.
Turn your ear to me;
  when I call, answer me quickly.

For my days vanish like smoke;
  my bones burn like glowing embers.
My heart is blighted and withered like grass;
  I forget to eat my food.
Because of my loud groaning
  I am reduced to skin and bones.
I am like a desert owl,
like an owl among the ruins.
I lie awake; I have become
  like a bird alone on a housetop.

Wet Evening in April

The birds sang in the wet trees
And as I listened to them it was a hundred years from now
And I was dead and someone else was listening to them.
But I was glad I had recorded for him
    The melancholy.

PATRICK KAVANAGH

■ Here is what happened halfway through my treatment for non-Hodgkin's Lymphoma in April 2006. I went for a midway scan to report on the shrinkage of my tumour and was given the wrong results.

My tumour was in fact responding well to the chemotherapy treatment I was being given. But the radiologist who analysed my scan pictures somehow looked at them the wrong way round, so mistakenly saw evidence of my tumour growing. I was told this meant it was not responding to treatment, and that a new, much harsher, course of chemotherapy would have to be put in place for me.

My family and I lived with the "truth" of this misdiagnosis for nine days until the mistake was uncovered. In that time we did our best to commit to ordinary life as best we could, doing the school run, eating and watching crap telly together, as you do. I do know I began writing my funeral service. I even broke the habit of a lifetime and discussed money with my wife.

During this time I was glad to come across this poem by Patrick Kavanagh. It became a kind of touchstone, helping me to come to terms with my forthcoming oblivion in language that was even more direct than my doctors'.

Let's Celebrate

the moments
where nothing happens.
The moments
that fill our lives.
Not the field bright with poppies, but
the times you walked, seeing
no leaves, no sky, only one foot
after another.

We are sleeping
(it's not midnight and
there is no dream).
We enter a room – no one is in it.
We run a tap,
queue to buy a stamp.

These are the straw moments
that give substance
to our astonishments;
moments the homesick dream of;
the bereaved, the diagnosed.

MANDY COE
Clay (Shoestring Press, 2009)

■ I will forever be grateful to Emma Metcalfe for recommending Mandy Coe's wonderful book *Clay* after my recovery from cancer in 2007.

I was exhausted, physically and mentally. And I could not understand why I kept wanting to cry in public places.

Without overstating it, I do think that, along with a small number of other books of poems, *Clay* is what got me reading poetry again. If you have not seen it, please check it out, you will not be sorry.

For one thing, Mandy does great titles. 'Sunflower Sex', anyone? 'Creationist Homework'? 'Sometimes It Occurs to Me That I Am Dead'?

For another thing, Mandy Coe is an original. No one looks at and writes about the world like she does. 'Stair-space is mysterious; / altering time and matter' she says in one poem ('You Only Notice Stairs During Strange Times'). In another poem a gecko 'pauses, receiving'. I love the minute attention to detail in that line, an almost Blakean sense of the divine in living things.

Everything in Mandy's world seems light. This is not to say she is not serious. I think everything Mandy writes is deadly serious, but wearing a grin and a cackle. Her project I think is to notice absolutely everything; not to do so, she seems to be saying, is not to live properly.

Which brings me to the perfect and devastating poem 'Let's Celebrate'. As I say, when I first read it I was still feeling my way into recovery and "normal" life, including that of work. If I am honest I found it hard to believe that my diagnosis and treatment had happened to me. I could not believe that the world seemed to have gone on perfectly well without me contributing to it in any significant way other than to shuffle with my son backwards and forwards to his primary school.

When I reached the end of the poem I actually felt winded. Few poems have the power both to acknowledge life *in extremis* while offering a vision of how it might be otherwise. I think Yeats called this a possession of both 'reality and justice'.

All I want to say to Mandy, and to her wonderful poem and book of poems, is thank you for noticing, and in noticing, giving me time to notice what is around me, even when 'nothing' is happening.

Era

The twenty-second day of March two thousand and three
I left home shortly after eight thirty
on foot towards the City. I said goodbye
to the outside of my body: I was going in.
The magpies were squabbling in the park.
The little fountain splashed chemical bubbles
over its lip. Traffic swarmed and swam
round Vauxhall Cross, like crazy fish, with teeth.

And anything could be real in a country
where Red Kites were spreading east and now
we had February swallows. Planes for Heathrow
roared not far enough overhead, shedding
jet trails which pointed over there: those other
places where all the frontiers end with a question.

JO SHAPCOTT
Of Mutability (Faber & Faber, 2011)

■ Really good books about cancer are rare. Really great books about cancer, the ones that offer new perspectives and change the language with which we discuss the disease, are even rarer.

Of Mutability is one of these books.

I came across 'Era' in reviewing *Of Mutability* for *The North* magazine in 2010. I began reading the book as news about it was beginning to spread. By the time my review was published it had won the Costa Book of the Year Award.

What struck me about the book, and why it will go on being so special, is the deliberate and cool detachment with which it is written. In one of the interviews she gave on winning the Costa, Shapcott was at pains to remind readers she was not an autobiographical writer 'to a point'. I think this helps explain why the

Costa judges prized *Of Mutability* as a 'paean to creativity', over and above its deft handling of the difficult subject-matter of cancer, a word the book never uses.

Readers will be aware, therefore, that Shapcott has never been a poet who bursts into the waiting room shouting about her issues and drawing attention to herself. And yet it is impossible not to talk about *Of Mutability* in the context of cancer, even though the book, like all great books, finally outstrips its subject-matter.

'Era' is the closest the book comes to putting on record what Thom Gunn called 'the sniff of the real' of what it is like to be treated for cancer. And yet the poem is not really "about" that at all. The date in the first line and the 'frontiers' in the last refer to Iraq: 2003 may have been a monumental year in the life of the speaker, but we are not allowed to forget that those 'jet trails', like those 'not far enough overhead' in London, brought and continue to bring dire consequences.

The 'squabbling' magpies, chemical fountains and traffic 'like crazy fish, with teeth' all presage more intimate transformations in the body. The speaker is admirably clear-eyed about this: it is a poem of 'goodbye' to things as they are. The implication is there will be no return to normal.

This tender-yet-tough tone runs throughout the collection as a whole. If you do not own a copy, I urge you to get your hands on one now. It takes a special kind of sensibility to link unasked-for changes in the body to global issues of the kind we find here, not least that of climate change, with 'red kites' 'spreading east' and 'February swallows'. The poem closes with a question but does not answer it. We leave the speaker poised on the edge of a new frontier, heading towards 'those other places', determined yet fragile, about to shed everything, 'over there'.

On the Impossibility of Staying Alive

They have found a new moon;
it stands on my shoulder.
They call it moon because
they lack imagination.
I call it moon because
I lack all conviction.

It has another name,
but that name, like God's
is terrible to pronounce.
It is terrible to pronounce
like Czrcbrno, a hamlet
in the Balkans. The moon
calls itself moon because
it lacks self-knowledge.

This moon sometimes whispers
and you never heard such rubbish.
I listen because I lack strength,
I smile because I have no muscles
with which to frown. At certain times
of the day, the moon hides.

When I am an old man
with flour in my beard, and
packs of incontinence pants
on the sideboard, the moon
will still be new, and will be
perpetually discovered as new
by generations of scientists.
The moon is not a nice man.

IAN McMILLAN
Selected Poems (Carcanet Press, 1990)

■ As Peter Sansom has said about Ted Hughes, until you have heard his voice, you are getting only two-thirds of him. This is how I feel about Ian McMillan. I had been enjoying his *Selected Poems* for a month or two, but it was not until I listened to a tape of him reading and introducing his poems in my car one summer that I fully comprehended what he was up to. Several of his phrases have ended up in my own private poetry-language: 'twist and reek', 'night's a dozen eggs', 'laughing like they laugh on radio plays', 'they hate poetry!'. Some of the titles of his poems dare you not to read them: 'The Red Indian Rugby Team 'Strange Names XV' Land on a Lonely Irish Beach'; 'Some Poetry Presses I Will Certainly Set Up in the Next Three Weeks'; 'Just the Facts, Just the'. Anyone who can describe Geoff Hattersley as 'Ezra Pound to my T.S. Eliot' is worth listening to and learning from.

Peter Sansom has written that McMillan's 'The Meaning of Life' might actually be about what it says it is, and that he realised this some ten years after first reading the poem. He also suggests that 'On the Impossibility of Staying Alive' could be titled 'Mortality', only that it would be much less interesting if it were. I am inclined to agree with this. On the one hand the poem is about Obviously Poetic Themes: 'God', 'the moon', 'imagination', 'self-knowledge', ageing and science. These are balanced with mentions of Not Obviously Poetic Material such as the hamlet 'Czrcbrno', sideboards and 'incontinence pants'.

However, I do not think this is an exercise in irony or faux-surreal juxtaposing. I think the terror of aging and death suffuse every syllable of this poem. I think McMillan has seen and felt enough of this world to know that death comes to most of us not as a romantic episode: it is literally 'terrible to pronounce'. This is why, just when the poem appears to relax into recognisably "poetic" statements, it immediately undercuts itself: 'This moon sometimes whispers / and you never heard such rubbish'. It takes both nerve and confidence to make such claims on the way to persuading us, in the poem's musical and unprovable final line, of the resilience of the human spirit, hinted at in the 'generations' of scientists in their dogged quest for discovery and illumination.

‘Questions unanswered’

Aunt Julia

Aunt Julia spoke Gaelic
very loud and very fast.
I could not answer her –
I could not understand her.

She wore men's boots
when she wore any.
– I can see her strong foot,
stained with peat,
paddling with the treadle of the spinningwheel
while her right hand drew yarn
marvellously out of the air.

Hers was the only house
where I've lain at night
in the absolute darkness
of a box bed, listening to
crickets being friendly.

She was buckets
and water flouncing into them.
She was winds pouring wetly
round house-ends.
She was brown eggs, black skirts
and a keeper of threepennybits
in a teapot.

Aunt Julia spoke Gaelic
very loud and very fast.
By the time I had learned
a little, she lay
silenced in the absolute black
of a sandy grave
at Luskentyre.

But I hear her still, welcoming me
with a seagull's voice
across a hundred yards
of peatscrapes and lazybeds
and getting angry, getting angry
with so many questions
unanswered.

NORMAN MacCAIG

The Many Days: Selected Poems of Norman MacCaig (Polygon, 2011)

■ Norman MacCaig's 'Aunt Julia' was the first poem I remember reading which made me think 'I need to do this'. I was about 14 at the time.

I'd been excited by Ted Hughes's early animal poems, Roger McGough's '40 Love', and John Logan's marvellous 'The Picnic'. The difference with 'Aunt Julia' was that I came upon it in the first book of poetry I had bought with my own money, Geoffrey Summerfield's *Worlds*.

It spoke to me immediately. I also had relations I could not converse with, my mother's family, French-speaking Swiss. We did French at school, of course, but it only made things worse. Here at last was a poem that validated my own speechless frustration.

When I read it now it is the simplicity of the language which continues to delight my nervous system, to borrow from Seamus Heaney. It pulls off the difficult trick of telling the reader as much about the speaker of the poem as it does its subject. Aunt Julia comes back to life through the poem's benign metaphorical gaze which draws attention to its artifice both as a remembered thing and its cry of lament for a lost way of life :

> She was buckets
> and water flouncing into them.
> She was winds pouring wetly
> round house-ends.
> She was brown eggs, black skirts
> and a keeper
> of threepennybits in a teapot.

I love his use of adverbs: 'marvellously' and 'wetly' are strange, but generous and exact. I love 'the absolute darkness / of a box bed, listening to/crickets being friendly.' They didn't have crickets in the Jura but the darkest room I ever slept in was at my grand-parents' house in La Chaux da Fonds. I dreamt that my fear and incomprehension could be similarly soothed by such insistent primitive music. And I love her 'threepenny bits / in a teapot' which seemed to conjure my grandmother's secret frugality precisely.

It is the poem that got me writing because it appeared when I needed it, (which wasn't till after I had read it). It told a story – while leaving most of the 'questions unanswered'; and because it taught me that plain language can be heart-breaking too.

I feel I owe it everything.

Swineherd

When all this is over, said the swineherd,
I mean to retire, where
Nobody will have heard about my special skills
And conversation is mainly about the weather.

I intend to learn how to make coffee, as least as well
As the Portuguese lay-sister in the kitchen
And polish the brass fenders every day.
I want to lie awake at night
Listening to cream crawling to the top of the jug
And the water lying soft in the cistern.

I want to see an orchard where the trees grow in straight lines
And the yellow fox finds shelter between the navy-blue trunks,
Where it gets dark early in summer
And the apple-blossom is allowed to wither on the bough.

EILÉAN NÍ CHUILLÉANAIN

Selected Poems (Gallery Press, 2008) by permission of the author and The Gallery Press, Loughcrew, Oldcastle, County Meath, Ireland.

■ I came across 'Swineherd' in quick succession via friends, workshops, anthologies and even newspaper columns, towards the end of the 90s. As one of a series of poem-posters produced by the Poetry Society, and thanks to the generosity of Siân Hughes, it now sits on the wall of my office at work.

Being aware of a poem's popularity or ubiquity has never been a good reason, in my book at least, to suddenly disown it. In the case of 'Swineherd', though I look at it most days, I am no nearer to guessing the veracity of story it tells, nor uncovering its every layer of meaning. Long before I read Ruth Padel's consummate reading of the poem in *The Independent*, I felt the poem nagging away at me with its combination of slushy consonants chiming off each other ('special'/'polish'), and the curtness of its 'c' sounds ('skills', 'coffee', 'fox', 'cream', 'crawling').

This push-and-pull sense of being teased was present all the way through the poem: What are the 'skills' which are so 'special'? Who is the 'Portuguese lay-sister'? What breed of 'yellow' fox are we talking about? Where (and why) does it get dark early in the summer? After a thousand readings, I still don't know.

The joy of it is that I don't need to, either. I have decided to savour the poem instead, to let it work on me as pure imagination. I allow it to create a space in which those possibly endangering 'special skills' (informer? torturer? bomber?), albeit retired, have come to rest in a place of order ('straight lines') which is itself threatened with the unexpected and the exotic ('yellow fox', 'navy-blue trunks'). The poem could be the all-time great riddling poem of The Troubles. Or it might be an answer to the dogmatic need, in all of us, for an 'answer' in the first place. It might be an argument for the primary function of art to create and then exist on a plane of its own logic and making. It might be all three.

'Underneath the mathematics of time'

Underneath the mathematics of time
was a theatre
around the corner from the ballerina statues
where the gradients covered India
next door to the flowers
who danced with the drill
where the Impressionists used spiky yellow art
where the language of education sat scribbling with delight

ANONYMOUS 10-YEAR-OLD GIRL

■ Phil Bowen gave me this poem, written by a ten-year-old girl, in 1998 to illustrate a writing game he submitted for *The Poetry Book for Primary Schools*. Siân Hughes and I called his exercise 'Under the Heart of the Sun'.

Phil's idea was based on the concluding poem of Simon Armitage's *Cloudcuckooland*, the one beginning 'under the bullet hole of the moon'. Taking suggestions from children, he draws up lists of words in three columns on the board.

First he collects images from the classroom environment: desks, waste paper baskets, computer screens, Viking posters etc. Next he takes 'big picture' words and phrases: images from nature and the world: the solar system, planets, oceans, names of rivers, mountain ranges and so on.

Finally he makes a list of prepositions, formal ones to start with (next to, underneath, alongside, below, inside etc.), then more idiomatic ones such as next door to, around the corner from etc.

The fun starts when you start blending these together to make new and extraordinary metaphors which may (or may not) make sense:

> Behind the Viking ship of the clouds
> Next to the dustbin of the sky
> Inside the ripped poster of the rain
> Behind the stop sign of the night

The resulting poems do not need to make narrative or linear sense. The purpose of the exercise is to see where the language takes you. It hasn't got to tell a story.

To illustrate his idea Phil sent me the poem above. Whenever I read it to teachers and children, they always look puzzled. But they also say how much they love its final line. We would love to scribble with delight as well, they say.

And I tell them that they can.

In the Desert Knowing Nothing

Here I am in the desert knowing nothing,
here I am knowing nothing
in the desert of knowing nothing,
here I am in this wide
desert long after midnight

here I am knowing nothing
hearing the noise of the rain
and the melt of fat in the pan

here is our man on the phone knowing something
and here's our man fresh from the briefing
in combat jeans and a clip microphone
testing for sound,
catching the desert rain, knowing something,

here's the general who's good with his men
storming the camera, knowing something
in the pit of his Americanness
here's the general taut in his battledress
and knowing something

here's the boy washing his kit in a tarpaulin
on a front-line he knows from his GCSE
coursework on Wilfred Owen
and knowing something

here is the plane banking,
the *go go go* of adrenalin
the child melting
and here's the grass that grows overnight
from the desert rain, feeling for him
and knowing everything

and here I am knowing nothing
in the desert of knowing nothing
dry from not speaking.

HELEN DUNMORE

Out of the Blue: Poems 1975-2001 (Bloodaxe Books, 2001).

■ I heard this poem before I ever read it, on one of those tapes the Poetry Society's education department used to produce to encourage children and teachers to listen to poetry. This was in the days before the Poetry Archive and Michael Rosen in your classroom at the touch of a button.

As I remember the tape included one of Michael's riffs about car journeys with his brother, and Jackie Kay's 'Sassenachs', One Of My All-Time Favourite Poems. Then this. No introduction, no context, the voice on the tape went straight in.

Perhaps that was the point. The context, the point, was everywhere. We had had Iraq#1 and were about to have #2. We knew about 'Stormin' Norman Schwarzkopf. We had witnessed children melting on the news. Nothing needed to be said.

And yet the poem isn't journalism. It takes you into the interior 'desert of knowing nothing', hundreds of miles from suffering, in a room where 'fat in the pan' is the closest to heat and to danger the speaker comes. Even with 'the noise of the rain' there is dryness, transmuted into a kind of spiritual ache for truth which 24-hour news coverage cannot sate.

The poem is bigger than its occasion, of course. In the years since I first heard it I have come to see it as a prophetic cry railing at the culture of 'clip microphones' and 'combat jeans', the glorification of war 'briefings' which are 'taut' with the self-importance of 'knowing' more than the viewer at home. Never has male hegemony been more finely skewered.

The rage it communicates can be applied to the march of neoliberal thought in more than military operations, however. Picture a reporter standing outside a hospital, or a school, where some alleged scandal has just taken place. Then picture those on the other side of the fence, now part of the discourse of derision taking place on their doorstep, their mouths complicit and 'dry', whether they speak up or not.

The Ingredient

Teacups have it.
I don't know why teacups have it,
but teacups do.
Horses turned out into a cold field have it,
as do the smouldering remains of a bonfire.
Mugs do not have it. That's a certainty.
Sacks of coal at the back gate have it,
and jig-saw puzzles have it,
and a river meandering through life has it.
A canal seems to have it, but it hasn't.
A bike has it, if it is a very very old bike.
Coloured pencils have it.
Leg irons are said to have it, but that's a joke,
and a very cruel joke at that.
This hasn't got it, but neither has a bottle of turps.
A Del Shannon 45 on the London label has it,
although a compilation LP of his Greatest Hits
doesn't have it even though it's tried really hard.
Ham salad has it.
Or rather, ham salad can have it but it doesn't always.
Leather gauntlets have it, if they are brown leather gauntlets.
Discarded silk at the foot of the bed doesn't have it,
although sometimes it's worth pretending that it does.
Night has it, if it has been snowing.
The sea has it, even though it is saddened by oil,
and I am happy to live by the sea.
Aircraft do not have it.
Parks used to have it, but most have lost it
and are unlikely to regain that which has been squandered.
But ducks and swans have it. Especially swans.
And certain dreams have it.
Not all dreams, but certain dreams.
Some photographs have it.
Some photographs do not.

You do not have it, but not having it is not everything.
I rarely have it, and even when I do
it seems as if I am not quite myself.
Perhaps this explains how come teacups have it
and mugs do not.

MARTIN STANNARD

The Gracing of Days (Slow Dancer, 1989) by permission of the author.

■ I first came across 'The Ingredient' in the library at the Totleigh Barton writing centre in Devon. The then centre director was having a bit of a spring clean, and I picked up *The Gracing of Days*, where this comes from, and *Denying England* (Wide Skirt), for virtually nothing.

I couldn't believe my luck. I had driven out there especially for a house warming for the new centre directors. Though I live in Devon I was new to the area and had got lost and was a bit frazzled on arriving. My children, who were young at the time, had accompanied me, and they were frazzled as well.

While they set about eating all the crisps I picked up Martin's book at random, having enjoyed his work in magazines. I found 'The Ingredient'. I have set about finding his work, by foul means or fair, ever since. I do happen to think he is a genius.

Martin is a bit like Paul Scholes in that he has been plying his trade in plain view for ages now (at least the duration of Scholes' 17-year career), but mostly unfêted and unloved, in contrast to Manchester's finest. Had he come from New York, or Zagreb, we would *all* be calling him a genius by now. But he isn't, and we don't. I know virtually nothing about him, except that he lived in Notts for a bit, and may well now be teaching and living in China. Or not.

I can't define my experience of 'The Ingredient' (and countless of Martin's other poems), except to say that I love being and living while I am reading and experiencing it. The pleasure pulses through my veins, you might say. It makes me smile, even though I will go to my grave knowing no more of why teacups have it and mugs do not.

The Only Son at the Fish 'n' Chip Shop

He lived with his mother till he was forty-five
and no one was allowed to touch his head.

He worked on a novel for twenty years
without writing a word. He didn't like people

who worked on novels. He often drank. One glass of beer
was too many, two glasses weren't enough.

Travel brochures were as far as he went.
A football match, one time. He often said

'Why would anyone want to think about a potato?'
He painted his door with nobody's help.

GEOFF HATTERSLEY
Back of Beyond: New & Selected Poems (Smith/Doorstop, 2006)

■ This devastating ten-line poem by Geoff Hattersley is living proof of the effect that good poems can have. As Peter Sansom once said about Deborah Randall, it achieves in a few lines what might take paragraphs in a novel. (Not that we don't like novels. We just prefer poems. For they are the real thing.)

And the Real Thing is absolutely what 'The Only Son at the Fish 'n' Chip Shop' is. There is context and setting (the eponymous shop; the mother). There is unfulfilled ambition (the novel in progress); there are habits (the drinking, the novel again); and there are attitudes: the dislike of 'people / who worked on novels' and being touched on the head.

Then there are those four extraordinary final lines, describing without sentimentality or condescension a life lived within the narrowest of limits. What makes these harrowing is the sense that the actions described within them, while in the past or continuous past tense, still persist in the present, unchanged and unchanging. This is alleviated, very briefly, by the oddness and spoken humour of that line about potatoes. Crucially, it takes the poem and the 'son' away from caricature and into actuality.

The Dog

I called amazon dot com and entered 'Robert Frost';
his hoary name a birch tree in a disco amid the graphics.
Working down the list I spotted the cassette tapes
and bounced my electric order off the satellite to Seattle.
They arrived shrink wrapped from their traverse
of the North Pole in the belly of a Boeing
and I took them on the M25 to Chelmsford.
Passing Potters Bar, with St Albans Cathedral
a squat blue bedstead on the west horizon
I listened to 'Death of a Hired Man',
the tape unspooling that ponderous conversation.
Then just before the tunnel with ceiling tracer sodiums:
'Trees at my window, window tree, my sash is lowered.'
and behind and beyond the raspy, old man's voice,
a faint dog bark out in the Massachusetts night.
It couldn't be caught, wouldn't be edited out;
barking at house lights maybe or a passing car
or rustlings from the shadows at the end of a yard,
defiant animus behind a mesh of wires.

CHRISTOPHER NORTH
A Mesh of Wires (Smith/Doorstop, 1999)

■ Occasionally the entrance of a poem into your life is a combination of a series of tiny events, each of them like a link in a chain which in hindsight appears inevitable.

Finding Christopher North's 'The Dog' was like this for me.

First of all I received an email from a friend telling me his pamphlet *A Mesh of Wires* was extremely good and that I should buy it immediately. I ignored it, of course.

Not so long afterwards I noticed that Christopher was going to be at the Ways With Words literature festival in Dartington, Devon.

I decided I would accidentally bump into him while I was there. This happened sooner than I had planned. There he was, in the oak-panelled dining room, holding court in a crumpled linen kind of way with some other writers I did not recognise. Knowing he would not know who I was, I froze and went to sit in the corner.

As luck would have it I found him later that afternoon leaning in a doorway I needed to go through. Pretending I did not need to go through it I approached him as though I had known I would find him there. He was at the festival to give his annual workshop on the art of keeping a notebook. Assuming flattery would get me everywhere, I asked him about it. The next hour or so flew by in a bespoke and personal tutorial on the great notebook keepers of the 20th century. He recommended *The Poet's Notebook: Excerpts from the Notebooks of Contemporary American Poets* (Norton, 1997), saying it was in the festival bookshop.

It wasn't. But lying on its own on a table there was *A Mesh of Wires*, ludicrously priced at £3. Decisions do not come much easier. I went back out to find Christopher so he could sign it, but he had vanished.

I ordered *The Poet's Notebook* on Amazon that night. Then I read *A Mesh of Wires* cover to cover, finishing with 'The Dog', marvelling at its combination of the actual and mysterious, its telepathic mirror image of my own actions a moment before. It's an experience I am still savouring.

Fishermen

the fishermen are patient
their lines settle in clear water
their wide-brimmed hats
will keep off
everything

on the boulevards meantime
carriages come and go
they carry
doctors to quiet basements
and children to circuses
music masters to doleful violins
and lovers to strange ceremonies
of whalebone and gardenias

the fishermen are unimpressed

over clear water
where the rod's end dances
the world is almost
under control

and everything that matters
is just
about to happen

ALASDAIR PATERSON

The Floating World: Selected Poems 1973-1982 (Pig Press, 1984) by permission of the author.

■ I first read 'Fishermen' as a newly qualified teacher, in Roger McGough's *Strictly Private* anthology (Puffin, 1985).

I love its patient and very filmic presentation of detail. Everything seems to have just the right weight. The tone is perfect, quiet yet oddly unsettling. Even more, I love that nothing in the poem is explained. We never find out what goes on in the 'quiet basements'; we never actually see the 'strange ceremonies'. And it seems every time I read it that the main action really is going on somewhere else, visible only to those 'umimpressed' fishermen.

It seems to me a miracle of restrained writing that is paradoxically very powerful. It entered my life at a time when I wanted to show poems to children that were full of accurately presented details which carried emotion in a direct and mysterious way. It is 20 plus years since I first encountered it, but its beauty and mystery have not dwindled for a second.

Psalm

How leaky are the borders of man-made states!
How many clouds float over them scot-free,
how much desert sand sifts from country to country,
how many mountain pebbles roll onto foreign turf
in provocative leaps!

Need I cite each and every bird as it flies,
or alights, as now, on the lowered gate?
Even if it be a sparrow – its tail is abroad,
thought its beak is still home. As if that weren't enough – it keeps
fidgeting!

Out of countless insects I will single out the ant,
who, between the guard's left and right boots,
feels unobliged to answer questions of origin and destination.

If only this whole mess could be seen at once in detail
on every continent!
Isn't that a privet on the opposite bank
smuggling its hundred-thousandth leaf across the river?
Who else but the squid, brazenly long-armed,
would violate the sacred territorial waters.?

How can we speak of any semblance of order
when we can't rearrange the stars
to know which one shines for whom?

Not to mention the reprehensible spreading of fog!
Or the dusting of the steppe over its entire range
as though it weren't split in two!
Or voices carried over accommodating air waves:
summoning squeals and suggestive gurgles!

Only what's human can be truly alien.
The rest is mixed forest, undermining moles, and wind.

WISŁAWA SZYMBORSKA

■ My edition of *Miracle Fair* contains a marvellous introduction to Wisława Szymborska's work by her compatriot Czesław Miłosz. Clear-sighted as the poetry he writes in praise of, he makes a number of startling observations which, had they been written by and about English poets, might have sparked a falling-out. (Who knows, maybe they did?) For example, he speaks of her poetry bringing 'joy because she is so sharp, because she derives pleasure out of juggling the props of our common heritage'. But only a sentence or two later goes on to state: 'To be frank, hers is a very grim poetry.'

I think it is perfectly possible to hold these apparently binary thoughts in tension. Elsewhere Miłosz explains the scientific-rationalist world-view that Szymborska inherited and was influenced by but never fully ascribed to. Her achievement, he claims, is to find for Polish poetry a method of 'existential meditation, leaving behind pure lyric and embarking on discourse'. The influence of 'biology lessons learned at school' may never be far behind, 'Yet she never makes the reductionist turn.'

This is a critical point and perhaps a counter-intuitive one: for the poems to work on us as 'discourse' they need first to work as poems. By all means let us remember the 'semblance of order' and 'the guard's left and right boots', but, like the psalmist of the poem's title, let us also consider the ant. Let us go further than that, into the realm of make-believe, childishness, even, and imbue it with consciousness.

It is the 'What if?' game played by all great poets (Kenneth Koch springs to mind). We know our history is terrible, but what if we could listen to the ant's perspective on it for a moment? The 'joy' is that the ant, like the poet, feels 'unobliged to answer'.

Down by the Station Early in the Morning

It all wears out. I keep telling myself this, but
I can never believe me, though others do. Even things do.
And the things they do. Like the rasp of silk, or a certain
Glottal stop in your voice as you are telling me how you
Didn't have time to brush your teeth but gargled with Listerine
Instead. Each is a base one might wish to touch once more

Before dying. There's the moment, years ago in the station in
Venice,
The dark rainy afternoon in fourth grade, and the shoes then,
Made of a dull crinkled brown leather that no longer exists.
And nothing does, until you name it, remembering, and even then
It may not have existed, or existed only as a result
Of the perceptual dysfunction you've been carrying around for years.
The result is magic, then terror, then pity at the emptiness,
Then air gradually bathing and filling the emptiness as it leaks,
Emoting all over something that is probably mere reportage
But nevertheless likes being emoted on. And so each day
Culminates in merriment as well as a deep shock like an electric one,

As the wrecking ball bursts through the wall with the bookshelves
Scattering the walls of famous authors as well as those
Of more obscure ones, and books with no author, letting in
Space, and an extraneous babble from the street
Confirming the new value the hollow core has again, the light
From the lighthouse that protects as it pushes away.

JOHN ASHBERY

■ I first read 'Down by the Station Early in the Morning' in Helen Vendler's *Faber Book of Contemporary American Poetry* (Faber & Faber, 1985). I seem to remember not having a clue what it was about but liking it very much indeed. It seems to me it might be one of the most beautiful poems ever written by anybody. It also seems to me very close to nonsense. That it inhabits the uncertain territory between dream and meaning is one of my chief pleasures when reading it.

I love it very much indeed.

There are reliable tropes of frustration, loss and melancholy: things 'wear out'; a 'dark rainy afternoon in fourth grade'; the 'perpetual dysfunction you've been carrying around for years'. A 'wrecking ball bursts through the wall… scattering works of famous authors'. It all seems very sad and dispiriting. And yet the tone is matter of fact, sunny even.

For what it is worth, my reading of the poem is this.

Abjuring the notion of the lyric as a trustworthy record of events, it seems instead to be an investigation into the reliability of the words we use to name the world around us. This is used, I think, to question the accuracy of the feelings we implicitly associate with them, and by implication the validity of using such source material – Venice in the early morning; going through fourth grade; 'the rasp of silk'– in poems that pertain to be personal.

I think the real action in the poem is away from those beautiful images of lighthouses and 'the glottal stop in your voice' and so on, but resides instead in words such as 'yes', 'instead', 'but', 'even', 'and', 'only' and 'as', in other words, the most basic connectives of all. These are used to create a kind of revolving door of images, metaphor seeding metaphor, until the self-doubt which is the genesis of the poem ('I can never believe me, though others do') in line 2, is forgotten.

I'm tempted to say the poem's final image, of the lighthouse protecting as it pushes away, could serve as a message to readers wanting to detect an autobiographical impulse, what the poem calls 'mere reportage', behind Ashbery's project. I could be wrong of course. I probably am. I don't really care. I invite others to come along and add their 'extraneous babble from the street.'

High Fidelity

The man sits above the tracks
at Bristol Parkway. He drinks tea,
studies the distance.
He notes the numbers of trains.

With the binocs he picks them out
on the long curve from Scotland,
the hard-driving run from Swindon.
He watches till the grey light fades.

He drinks tea and talks to himself
about the rude girls who serve him.
He takes some pills – perhaps the ones
the doctors make him take.

I note him down,
after my airport poems,
my studies of Sappho, Bathsheba,
and Sylvia Plath.

I ride one of his numbers home
impatient to be undisturbed with a malt
and my rank-ordering of all the available versions
of the Goldberg Variations,

BWV988.

CHRIS SOUTHGATE
Easing the Gravity Field: Poems of Love and Science (Shoestring Press, 2006)

■ I first heard Chris Southgate's 'High Fidelity' sometime in 2005, when I was lucky enough to be part of a writers' group with him.

The day Chris brought 'High Fidelity' was special, because I had the rare impression of hearing perfect art straight off the cuff as it were. When he finished reading my own response went something along the lines of – there is nothing to change, it's done.

You can find it in his 2006 collection *Easing the Gravity Field: Poems of Science and Love*. I don't think it has changed much, not that it needed to.

I love everything about this poem, from its calculated yet non-judgemental observations to its relish of language, and, by implication, finding the extraordinary in the ordinary. I love its humour – like Chris when you meet him, of the driest and most self-effacing kind, gently poking fun at the enterprise of note taking and writing poetry. I love the twist in the isolated final line, the link it makes to the man at the railway station; I love the community of this, and the silence.

If you do not know Chris's work, I urge you to get hold of it. His recent *A Gash in the Darkness* (Shoestring) is just as good: wry, compassionate, and brimming with mystery. I should add that he is a wonderful reader of his work, really taking time to give his words space to breathe: if you have not heard him, you are in for a treat.

Nightwatchman

Mouth set. So far, nought
not out, having dabbed at
the spinner who'd been giving it
some air. Hands soft – taking the sting
out of each delivery.

Their demon quickie
is brought back into the attack.
                    He pounds in.
A virtuoso leave.
                          You judge the away
swinger to perfection.

Shadows nudge further east
across the square. Pigeons clatter
as mid-off jogs back. Thunderous
approach to the wicket. This one
you nick.
                The keeper whoops and hurls
the ball to the skies. You walk without waiting,
head-down to a door marked VISITORS.

In among the grim socks, grass-stained whites
and open coffins you take in
the smell of embrocation, shake off
gloves, stoop to unbuckle your pads.

PETER CARPENTER
Just Like That (Smith/Doorstop, 2012)

■ I met Peter Carpenter in the summer of 2001 at the Arvon Foundation's Totleigh Barton writing centre. I was at a low ebb of writing at the time. I had published one book of poems, in 1996. In spite of that book's relative success my publisher had no plans to do a follow-up second collection. I had been sending my second manuscript to publishers for several months, collecting many polite notes of rejection in the process.

I felt as if I was about to drop off the face of the earth.

One week after the Arvon course finished Peter emailed me to ask if I had a manuscript of poems that I might be prepared to send to him at Worple Press. One week later he said that he liked it very much and would like to publish it the following year. Since that moment, and very often since, I have felt that I owe him my life. My utter and profound feeling of despondency was replaced in an instant by one of relief.

I think of Peter as an angel and Worple as home.

So, being honest, I am biased when I read his poems. I come to them knowing his voice and his poetics and the rhythm of his thinking. You could say I am on his side, before I even turn the page. This feeling is doubled when the poem in question is about cricket and is subtitled 'an elegy'. (We all have our prejudices, consciously or not; W.H. Auden encourages us to admit them frankly.)

Carpenter does silence brilliantly: the silence between people, the silence of crowds at football and at the racing, the silence of defeat:

> In among the grim socks, grass-stained whites
> and open coffins, you take in
> the smell of embrocation, shake off
> gloves, stoop to unbuckle your pads.

Like all good poems, 'Nightwatchman' is about much more than what it is about. The 'dreaded finger', the 'marked' door and open coffins (kitbags) of team-mates all point towards death. Carpenter's chief tactic, however, is not to persuade the reader of this but to present these luminous details – which point towards loss – with control and tact. Poem after poem in *Just Like That*, from which this poem comes, accomplishes the feat of leaving the reader meditating on the strangeness of what has been described in measured syntax and precisely rendered detail.

‘Heavens, I recognise the place,
I know it!’

Poem

About the size of an old-style dollar bill,
American or Canadian,
mostly the same whites, gray greens, and steel grays
– this little painting (a sketch for a larger one?)
has never earned any money in its life.
Useless and free, it has spent seventy years
as a minor family relic
handed along collaterally to owners
who looked at it sometimes, or didn't bother to.

It must be Nova Scotia; only there
does one see gabled wooden houses
painted that awful shade of brown.
The other houses, the bits that show, are white.
Elm trees, low hills, a thin church steeple
– that gray-blue wisp – or is it? In the foreground
a water meadow with some tiny cows,
two brushstrokes each, but confidently cows;
two minuscule white geese in the blue water,
back-to-back, feeding, and a slanting stick.
Up closer, a wild iris, white and yellow,
fresh-squiggled from the tube.
The air is fresh and cold; cold early spring
clear as gray glass; a half inch of blue sky
below the steel-gray storm clouds.
(They were the artist's specialty.)
A specklike bird is flying to the left.
Or is it a flyspeck looking like a bird?

Heavens, I recognise the place, I know it!
It's behind – I can almost remember the farmer's name.
His barn backed on that meadow. There it is,
titanium white, one dab. The hint of steeple,
filaments of brush-hairs, barely there,

must be the Presbyterian church.
Would that be Miss Gillespie's house?
Those particular geese and cows
are naturally before my time.

A sketch done in an hour, 'in one breath,'
once taken from a trunk and handed over.
Would you like this? I'll probably never
have room to hang these things again.
Your Uncle George, no, mine, my Uncle George,
he'd be your great-uncle, left them all with Mother
when he went back to England.
You know, he was quite famous, an R.A....

I never knew him. We both knew this place,
apparently, this literal small backwater,
looked at it long enough to memorise it,
our years apart. How strange. And it's still loved,
or its memory is (it must have changed a lot).
Our visions coincided – 'visions' is
too serious a word – our looks, two looks:
art 'copying from life' and life itself,
life and the memory of it so compressed
they've turned into each other. Which is which?
Life and the memory of it cramped,
dim, on a piece of Bristol board,
dim, but how live, how touching in detail
– the little that we get for free,
the little of our earthly trust. Not much.
About the size of our abidance
along with theirs: the munching cows,
the iris, crisp and shivering, the water
still standing from spring freshets,
the yet-to-be-dismantled elms, the geese.

ELIZABETH BISHOP

The Complete Poems, 1927-1979 (Farrar, Straus & Giroux, New York, 1983)

■ The funniest thing you will ever read about Elizabeth Bishop (or teaching, or anything else) is Mark Halliday's essay 'Moose Failure'. In it Halliday presents the idea that sometimes even very great poems do not work in the classroom, however intelligent the students, however careful the planning and wonderful the ideas of the teacher concerned.

This had been my experience of Elizabeth Bishop, until I came across 'Poem' in Helen Vendler's *Faber Book of Contemporary American Poetry*. I had read Bishop before, of course, but felt I had not properly connected with her.

I felt she belonged to other people, not me. I knew other people had forged this connection as I kept meeting her in workshops ('Sestina', 'One Art'), the poems of other poets ('Skunk Hour') and in essays ('The Government of the Tongue'). But all I felt was failure. Moose Failure. I did not need to be persuaded of her greatness, I just wanted to find a connection.

More on a whim than a recommendation I picked up the Faber anthology and began reading Helen Vendler's clear-sighted Introduction. The essay ends with a brief overview of 'Poem'. Twice she quotes what seems to me the poem's central line and turning point: 'Heavens, I recognise the place, I know it!', the second of these followed by this bombshell of plain-speaking:

> It is the effect every poet hopes for; and, to be complete, it must be followed by that other, estranging effect which tells us, by style, that the elms in the poem are, by their placement in the virtual world of language, already dismantled and gone.

This seemed to be someone who I both wanted and now needed to do business with.

As Vendler points out the poem enacts its own meaning by presenting the 'stages by which we enter a work of art': indifference; recognition of generic features or of its making ('fresh-squiggled from the tube'); sudden and emotional recognition ('I know it!'); and finally the personal, which may also contain moral responses and those tinted with regret ('the yet-to-be-dismantled elms, the geese').

I turned to the poem and read it knowing I already loved it, having been set up to by Vendler's exposition. Then I read her essay again, and then the poem, noting on a scrap of paper which

I have now lost these lines:

> The poem stands before us brilliantly photographic and brilliantly verbal at once. If it were not also (to paraphrase Lowell) a shape solid with yearning and written in light, a shape formed by both heart and mind, it would expend its mimetic and verbal energies in vain.

I love 'Moose Failure'. But I love this more.

The Way We Live

Pass the tambourine, let me bash out praises
to the Lord God of movement, to Absolute
non-friction, flight, and the scarey side:
death by avalanche, birth by failed contraception.
Of chicken tandoori and reggae, loud, from tenements,
commitment, driving fast and unswerving
friendship. Of tee-shirts on pulleys, giros and Bombay,
barmen, dreaming waitresses with many fake-gold
bangles. Of airports, impulse, and waking to uncertainty,
to strip-lights, motorways, or that pantheon –
the mountains. To overdrafts and grafting

and the fit slow pulse of wipers as you're
creeping over Rannoch, while the God of moorland
walks abroad with his entourage of freezing fog,
his bodyguard of snow.
Of endless gloaming in the North, of Asiatic swelter,
to launderettes, anecdotes, passions and exhaustion,
Final Demands and dead men, the skeletal grip
of government. To misery and elation; mixed,
the sod and caprice of landlords.
To the way it fits, the way it is, the way it seems
to be: let me bash out praises – pass the tambourine.

KATHLEEN JAMIE

Mr & Mrs Scotland Are Dead: Poems 1980-1994 (Bloodaxe Books, 2002).

■ Sometimes you do not get a poem, or what a poet is up to, straight away. In the case of Kathleen Jamie's wonderful 'The Way We Live' I needed three goes before it broke over me like an egg.

Not for one second do I think this the fault of the poem.

My first encounter with it was through Neil Astley's anthology *Poetry with an Edge*, published in 1988. The book came into my life at a time when reading and writing poems seemed as important as breathing. This was mixed with the giddiness of sleepless nights in the early stages of childcare, a heady cocktail, and not always conducive to optimal concentration.

This isn't special pleading, this is just how it was.

Still in that phase of trying to find and create art in the cracks between working and late night feeding, I found *The Way We Live* (Bloodaxe Books, 1987) in a second-hand bookshop in Teignmouth in the autumn of 1995. We were living in London at the time, and, though we did not know it, had begun to feel the pull of the west country, where we now live.

If I am honest, 'The Way We Live' passed me by; I was more taken with the poems in the book's first section, especially 'November'.

'The Way We Live' finally came into my life in October 1998, at the Arvon Foundation's Lumb Bank writing centre. With Siân Hughes, I had been asked to fill the "in loco parentis" role for prizewinning young poets who were being tutored by Jo Shapcott and Roger McGough, for the first ever Foyle Young Poets Award (then called the Simon Elvin Young Poets Award).

As I remember it Jo led a workshop on writing poems of praise and curses. I will always be grateful to Jo that one of the models we worked from was 'The Way We Live'.

I loved its energy and fusing together of disparate elements to make a coherent whole:

> Of chicken tandoori and reggae, loud, from tenements,
> commitment, driving fast and unswerving
> friendship.

That seems witty to me, both deeply felt and light. What a masterstroke of control to place the notion of 'unswerving' after 'driving fast', and linking it, over the cliff fall of a line break, to 'friendship'.

Book-ended with instructions to 'pass the tambourine', I don't think it is overstating it to say the poem is Psalm-like in its intense cataloguing of experience. Creativity-theorists call this kind of openness 'over-inclusivity'. The poem thus records and is a record of the necessary and sometimes extreme receptivity required to get a piece of work or project completed.

I suspect its lack of judgementalism played a key role in appealing to those young writers that day. The poem presents and accumulates details in a continuous present tense; it does not commentate. In this way I suspect it spoke to them of who they were at that time, as it were holding up a mirror to their lives: here is a poem by a young person: you can do this too! Watching them love it, I loved it.

Prayer

Every day I want to speak with you. And every day something
more important
calls for my attention – the drugstore, the beauty products, the
luggage

I need to buy for the trip.
Even now I can hardly sit here

among the falling piles of paper and clothing, the garbage trucks
outside
already screeching and banging.

The mystics say you are as close as my own breath.
Why do I flee from you?

My days and nights pour through me like complaints
and become a story I forgot to tell.

Help me. Even as I write these words I am planning
to rise from the chair as soon as I finish this sentence.

MARIE HOWE

The Kingdom of Ordinary Time (W.W. Norton, 2008) by permission of W.W. Norton & Company, Inc.

■ I first came across 'Prayer' next to an interview with the poet in the Poetry Trust's *Poetry Paper*.

It knocked me sideways.

First, I love the clarity of its language. Second, I admire its tackling of complex spiritual material without sounding coy, ironic or mystical. Even though mysticism is directly referred to in the poem, the actual world of the poem remains grounded in the here and now of travel, appointments and 'garbage trucks'. It is the apparently unresolvable tension between these pressing realities and the call of something other on the speaker's attention that gives the poem its energy.

I love this poem of spiritual longing. I have cut it out and attached it to the shelf above my desk. I lift my eyes from my screen and it hangs there, silently rebuking me. Yet even as I type these words I wonder if I should be checking my Twitter account for an update of the *News of the World* scandal.

Sunday Lunchtime

The whirlpools of the launderette
do not recognise the Sabbath,

so the air in Worple Street
smells of soapsuds and roast beef.

The Church of Healing is silent
with endeavour – and the Oddfellows

have gathered in their Hall –
now they'll be there till evening.

Mr Patel leans on his counter
and reads about HEAVEN ON EARTH –

A celestial city discovered by *Sunday Sport*
as a change from sex. In the street

Concorde glides across car windows,
noisy as hell, but tiny as a paper dart.

CONNIE BENSLEY
Finding a Leg to Stand On: New & Selected Poems (Bloodaxe Books, 2012)

■ I first came across 'Sunday Lunchtime' in a copy of *Sunk Island Review*, edited by Michael Blackburn. You can find the poem in Connie Bensley's marvellous Bloodaxe selected, *Finding a Leg to Stand On*.

As I have said before, this was a period of my life when I subscribed to everything that moved, partly in the hope it would increase my chances of having my poems accepted. (For the record, this strategy never came close to working for *Sunk Island Review*, a fact I remain curiously proud of to this day.)

What struck me then and still gives pleasure now is the way the poem deals with difficult everyday material in an apparently artless fashion. Biblical and religious references share the same earth as the Sunday Sport, Concorde and corner shops. It is a perfect working model of propriety and tact.

I have used Bensley's poems 'The Star and the Birds' and 'Rust' as exemplars of writing which successfully blends imagery from two contrasting vocabularies. In 'Sunday Lunchtime' the 'whirlpools of the launderette' recall the miracle at the pool of healing at Bethesda in John's gospel. It comes as no surprise when 'The Church of Healing' itself is mentioned: this is a world where 'smells of soap-suds and roast beef' reside next to 'celestial' cities.

None of this would count for much, however, without the low-key exhilaration of the poem's final lines. The shift of perspective offered here is both sudden and deft. Concorde arrives silently across car windows and is caught up as it were by its own jet engines. Our most soaring and complex invention is reinvented 'tiny as a paper dart', a true and rueful coming back to earth born from a gaze that is heavenwards in reverse.

Eating Outside

Fat pine boughs
droop over the vegetable garden's
sticks and leaves,
the moon's hazy face comes and goes
in the heat.
Beautiful women,
your skin can barely be seen.
The moon's gone. Clouds everywhere.
A pale hand curls
on the tabletop next to mine,
there's talk about work and love.
We're like the moon at this hour
as clouds swallow it or dissolve so
it glides through the shaggy limbs,
full, like the grief inside us,
then floats off by itself
beyond the last tips of the needles.
The trees are quiet. In the house
my daughters play the piano and laugh.
The family dog races in and out howling.
The candles on the table have blown out.
I keep trying to explain
but when I go back, like now, there's
the red hammock, the barbecue guarding
the lit back wall like a dwarf,
the self, awed by changes,
motioning to us as it leaves.
Deep among those arms, it pauses
clear, white and unseen.

STEPHEN BERG

New & Selected Poems (Copper Canyon Press, USA, 1992).

■ Above the desk where I am writing this is a shelf on which sits more than a yard of poetry from North America.

I decided to move it into my office for practical reasons as much as anything. There just wasn't room for it to stay mixed in with everything from everywhere else. It seemed to demand its own space. It may one day need its own room. I like seeing it there, growing silently, year on year, like Sylvia Plath's mushrooms (which reminds me, for some reason she is in the wrong shelf, on her own with the Brits...).

There are books by Sharon Olds and Robert Lowell and Raymond Carver up there which seem to have been with me forever. Another book I seem to have always had is Stephen Berg's *New and Selected Poems*, published in the UK by Bloodaxe in 1992 and which I have just discovered you can buy on Amazon for 13p. Which seems to me both a bargain and something of a scandal. (If you look for him on the Bloodaxe site, he isn't there either. Maybe, as we used to say about indie bands in the 1980s, he has been "dropped"). A bargain, because 13p for 219 pages of amazing lyric poetry is a serious proposition, austerity or no. A scandal because I think he should be a household name, like Billy Collins and C.K. Williams.

Here, in fact, is what C.K. Williams has to say about him, on the back cover blurb:

> Passionate and audacious, eloquent and zany, Berg's poems deal with the most raw and emotionally rending themes, while maintaining a startling forthrightness of vision and a remarkable elegance of tone... This is the lyric striving to extend itself, and the human soul struggling to come to terms with all the lost and lonely corners of its mansion.

This is remarkable in the purple-prose world of poetry blurbs for being both selfless and true.

I read Stephen Berg's *New and Selected Poems* cover to cover, during the time in my life when I had made an active decision to put poetry at the heart of the enterprise of everything I was doing. Mostly this involved reading, secretly, and writing even more secretly, occasionally sending a poem to a magazine and losing weight while I waited for a response. This coincided with the birth of my children.

I am not sure how I heard about Stephen Berg's wonderful book. (If memory serves it was a review in *Scratch* magazine. Or perhaps it was a Bloodaxe catalogue.) But I did decide to buy it, and read it, and learn from it. I love his head-on tackling of difficult subject-matter. Far from feeling 'confessional' the poems sound to me as though he had no choice in the matter, simultaneously displaying self-awareness of the cost, both of writing them and concomitant silence. I think this is what people mean when they say a writer is up to the challenge of writing honestly about the age they happen to live in.

The book feels both weighty and slim. The titles of the poems ('William Carlos Williams Reading His Poems', 'Wanting to be Heavier', 'At a Friend's Birthday Party in the Garden at Night', 'Sunday Afternoon') draw you in and give you an immediate flavour of something both ordinary and mysterious. It contains two astonishing sequences: 'With Akhmatova at the Black Gates' and the sixteen-page *tour de force* 'Homage to the Afterlife', each line of which begins with the words 'Without me…'.

I thought about 'Eating Outside' this week as it is an activity I like doing and would like to be doing more of in this cursed British summer of ours. I admire its almost Chekhovian sensibility, with its cataloguing of 'beautiful women', 'talk about work and love' and overt symbolism of the moon. Much more than that, I am very taken with the way the poem begins with a plain description of 'fat pine boughs' to one of the 'self', twenty-eight lines later, as 'clear, white and unseen'.

Having spent time with this poem for twenty or so years, I am still not completely sure how this change is carried successfully into the ear and the mind of the reader. I do know that each time I read it, even though I know how the poem ends, these final lines seem to rise up out of somewhere very profound and unsettled. It is here, in a garden I know and have spent time in. You have been there as well.

How It All Started

Do you know this dream? An exam room
full of neat, serious girls, your lucky gonk
by your fountain pen, the plop of tennis balls
through an open window. You're here for
'O' Level history on The Causes
Of The First World War but you've no idea –
too busy bunking off to watch *Crown Court*,
and the teacher says *You may turn over*
and begin and there's a question
on the Algeciras crisis and all you can think is,
Algeciras sounds like a virus or a cloud formation,
your eyes blur, scanning for something
you understand, you wonder who Bismarck was,
why his web of Alliances was so significant,
your throat swells like a new loaf, you watch
the girls who know the answers to these things,
and you think of the stutter of gunfire, a soldier's
booted foot lying in a puddle, how the leather split,
how the rest of him wasn't there, just a stump
of bone, and if you'd learned how it all started,
you might have known how to prevent this.
You should have known how to prevent this.

CATHERINE SMITH
Lip (Smith/Doorstop, 2007)

■ Sometimes life on Planet Poetry is not all it is cracked up to be. The endless buying of books none of your relations or work colleagues have ever heard of. The attending of readings with 11 other people, down a lane, in a thunderstorm. The feeling of being pursued by a cloud which flashes a ten foot neon sign above your head saying I HAVE WASTED MY LIFE.

Or maybe you don't do the first two. Maybe that's just me.

Sometimes, this is all worthwhile.

You open, as my children would say, literally open a magazine, and there it is, the poem you have been looking for all your life (the one you may even be secretly trying to write, badly), a poem so right, so here and now in the present moment of your breathing and longing, it is as if you hear it in your very own voice, the one you pretend you know and love.

Opening *The Rialto* poetry magazine, literally, at my kitchen table, and finding 'How It All Started' by Catherine Smith, was such a moment for me.

The recognition, the yes, that's it exactly, please keep writing like this, of that one syllable time-bomb of 'gonk'. The way this rhymes and chimes (but not quite! brilliant!) with 'plop', underneath it (but not quite directly underneath it, kind of to the side, slant). The repetition of 'your', 'you' and 'you're', four times in four lines, taking you by the hand and immersing you in its dream-world. Those lines (but it does not say 'lines') of 'neat, serious girls'. That 'fountain pen'. You do not need to be a stationery-obsessive to know how devastatingly right that detail is. (But it helps.)

And we haven't even got to the content yet! Bismarck. The Algeciras crisis. That 'booted foot lying in a puddle'.

The heart-stopping brilliance (I actually – literally, I mean – think mine did) of 'your throat swells like a new loaf'.

All of this...all of this *life*! I pounded, hit my hand till it hurt, the kitchen table in excitement. Never mind that my own (bad) dream-exam poem was now redundant, *forever*. Never mind all that.

Here it was. In my house. A living, kicking, screaming, working-perfect, controlled-raw thing-artefact-poem expanding my life and renewing my faith in poems and art and learning (ironically).

Every single one of the poems in Catherine's astonishing book *Lip* is as good.

Coming Home

The bar is full of English cigarette smoke
and English voices, getting louder –
a language lumpy as a ploughed field.
It's hard to believe our tongues have got it too.

People are growing drunk at the thought of home.
The sea patiently knits its wide grey sleeve.
No one else comes up to lean on the rail
where, damp and silent, we watch

the long white skirts of land drifting
sadly through mist, as if a young girl sat
by the shore still, waiting for a bluebird.
It's September, and already winter.

And now the toy-sized train
is creeping with its worn-out battery
and a cargo of sandwiches and arguments
over grey-green fields into grey-white suburbs.

We're playing a game with the streets –
spreading them out and tying them up again;
when they've caught us, we're home.
The lawn blows like a tiny English Channel.

We chug towards our own front door
anxiously, seeing as if for the first time
how tight the plot that locks us in,
how small our parts, how unchosen.

CAROL RUMENS

Unplayed Music (Secker & Warburg, London, 1981) and *Poems 1968-2004* (Bloodaxe Books, 2004) by permission of the author.

■ When I first read 'Coming Home' in *The Penguin Book of Contemporary British Poetry* I entered it via my own memories of summer holidays on cross-Channel ferries, travelling to see and returning from seeing my mother's relatives in Switzerland. The bar 'full of English cigarette smoke' and 'language lumpy as a ploughed field', these are passages I have lived through, not to mention those lonely vigils leaning 'on the rail' and wanting to throw up over it.

As a young person from the 'suburbs' encountering new poems, I think this is what you do.

Reading it again now I enjoy the relish of those memories, included in which are the memories of first discovering the poem. I enjoy its low-key observations and empirically accumulated detail; I even accept the note of resignation in its final lines, with their knowing and complicit nod to the same in Larkin's 'Afternoons'. But I am reminded, too, of Frost's linkage of homecoming to composing lines of poetry: 'a poem begins as a lump in the throat, a homesickness, a lovesickness. It finds the thought and the thought finds the words'.

I cannot go back to my 21-year-old self and warn him that there is more to the world of poetry than *The Penguin Book of Contemporary British Poetry*. I would like to tell him to remain open to whatever poems come his way, and what is said about them. If I could I would tell him to read (and write) everything he gets his hands on, by whichever means the poems arrive or are recommended. I would tell him not to be afraid, and to follow his nose, for he has nothing to lose, even as he sees his 'own front door' 'as if for the first time' and considers his commonplace setting, however provincial and small.

A Poem for Someone Who Is Juggling Her Life

This is a poem for someone
who is juggling her life.
Be still sometimes.
Be still sometimes.

It needs repeating
over and over
to catch her attention
over and over,
because someone juggling her life
finds it difficult to hear.

Be still sometimes.
Be still sometimes.
Let it all fall sometimes.

ROSE COOK

Notes From a Bright Field (Cultured Llama, 2013), by permission of the author

■ To say I loved this poem immediately would be an understatement. It spoke into that place which exists, Frost says, 'before words were, living in the cave of the mouth'. It sent me back to myself and to silence, creating an unlooked for moment of repose in an otherwise hectic day.

It does this, I think, through its marvellous handling of tone. It manages to give instruction ('Be still sometimes'), and to repeat this, without for a second sounding didactic. It is as though the speaker addresses the reader like a patient senior family member, dropping their hands to the listener's shoulder and leaning in with advice, before turning away to utter the second stanza like an aside to an invisible audience. This contains the world-weary but loving tone of one who has seen it all before, yet who has managed not to let cynicism enter her heart.

The poem's last instruction, 'let it all fall sometimes', is a coming to and a blowing open, rather than a closing down. It urges the practising of acceptance, and as such brings to mind the aphoristic wisdom of religious poetry. It looks like the end of the argument, a poem which wants to have the final word. I think it is much more than that. It places the reader back in the centre of what happens, of what we know will happen and must happen, for "progress" to occur.

Song of Reasons

Because of the change of key midway in 'Come Back to Sorrento'
The little tune comes back higher, and everyone feels

A sad smile beginning. Also customary is the forgotten reason
Why the Dukes of Levis-Mirepoix are permitted to ride horseback

Into the Cathedral of Notre Dame. Their family is so old
They killed heretics in Languedoc seven centuries ago;

Yet they are somehow Jewish, and therefore the Dukes claim
Collateral descent from the family of the Virgin Mary.

And the people in magazines and on television are made
To look exactly the way they do for some reason, too:

Every angle of their furniture, every nuance of their doors
And the shapes of their eyebrows and shirts has its history

Or purpose arcane as the remote Jewishness of those far Dukes,
In the great half-crazy tune of the song of reasons.

A child has learned to read, and each morning before leaving
For school she likes to be helped through The Question Man

In the daily paper: Your Most Romantic Moment? Your Family Hero?
Your Worst Vacation? Your Favourite Ethnic Group? – and pictures

Of the five or six people, next to their answers. She likes it;
The exact forms of the ordinary each morning seem to show

An indomitable charm to her; even the names and occupations.
It is like a bedtime story in reverse, the unfabulous doorway

Of the day that she canters out into, businesslike as a dog
That trots down the street. The street: sunny pavement, plane trees,

The flow of cars that come guided by with a throaty music
Like the animal shapes that sing at the gates of sleep.

ROBERT PINSKY

The Figured Wheel: New & Collected Poems 1966–1996 (Farrar, Straus and Giroux, 1996; Carcanet Press, 1996) by permission of the publishers.

■ It is more than twenty years since I bought Peter Sansom's *Writing Poems*. Among that wonderful book's many delights I found recommendations of poets, their poems, books and anthologies. Somewhere near the back is a long list of the latter, among which features Helen Vendler's *Faber Book of Contemporary American Poetry* (Faber, 1986) – which I note you can now by on Amazon for 1p.

If you don't know it, get it. It's a great introduction to American poetry in the 20th century. It is not perfect (why it does not include Kenneth Koch and James Schuyler is beyond me), but it does remain one of my favourites for the simple reason that it came into my life at the time when I most needed it.

Not least among my reasons for loving and returning to it is my discovery in its pages of the work of Robert Pinsky. He is represented by a mere four poems in the book, but I would argue they are the ones which most knocked me sideways, not having come across his work before. The final poem in Vendler's selection is 'Song of Reasons'.

Some years after discovering this poem I took it to the writers' group I belonged to at the time. There followed quite a long disquisition into and explication of its features, I seem to recall. Was it the Modernist lyric being reinvented or something altogether more alluring? Interesting though this was, something about the discussion troubled me. Nowhere among our eloquent responses did any of us say how close to the pulse of actual thought the poem appears to be.

Reading it again today I am struck how the poem carefully balances out the twin impulses hinted at in its title, the human need for 'song' cantilevered by the rational mind of 'reasons'. Thus the poem presents 'arcane' and 'forgotten' facts about a French aristocratic family, their religions and customs. Humming around it is the trivia of everyday life, 'the change of key midway in "Come Back to Sorrento"', 'people in magazines and on television', a newspaper quiz and those cars with their 'throaty music'. I'm tempted to read a domestic scene into these details, of an 'ordinary' family breakfast perhaps.

In this way the poem contains what Les Murray once said all poetry had to have in order to be alive: the three elements of body, mind and dream. The latter is hinted at only in the poem's very final words, appearing as it were from behind 'gates' we are never admitted behind, a 'bedtime story in reverse' which is no less suggestive, or gorgeous, for that.

Boggle Hole

Two new mountain bikes chained to the fence,
three horses lean over, bite at the tyres,
get the chain between their teeth,
eat most of a saddle and a handlebar grip.

Boggle Hole Youth Hostel and someone
has written 'welcome to BOGGLE HELL'
on the bottom of the bunk above this one
in red felt tip and shaky writing.

A gang of bikers comes in late – a bottle
smashes outside the door then it's quiet
but for the talking, distorted, muffled
through the wall, apart from that voice…

After breakfast a tractor tows a boat
named *Freedom* into the sea. There used to be
smugglers here and someone wrote 'LULU'
four feet high in the slipway's wet concrete.

Freedom is oil-grey, just below the horizon
when a dog tears along sideways, its tongue out,
tasting the salt on the wind, and, in the first
drops of rain, a boy draws a donkey in the sand.

CLIFF YATES
Frank Freeman's Dancing School (The Knives Forks and Spoons Press, 2015)

■ If you do not know Cliff Yates's work, you could worse than start with *Frank Freeman's Dancing School*, from which 'Boggle Hole' comes. Reading them is a bit like watching the best kind of slapstick comedy: each gag is inevitable, hilarious and sad all at once. In his poems you see the wooden plank on the shoulder of one man as it spins around, misses his friend as he ducks out of the way then catches him in the face on the return circuit.

What Cliff also shows us, and this is what give the poems a special kind of resonance, is the following shot where you can catch the same man scrabbling around on the floor, looking for a contact lens, perhaps, or perhaps just scrabbling around on the floor. Cliff does not moralise or attempt to persuade us what this might mean.

'Boggle Hole' is funny, and lyrical and a bit sad all at once. I do think it displays Cliff's unique way of looking at and experiencing the world. I think the established trope to describe an oblique take on experience is now "surreal". This is not quite true of Cliff, since his poems are not voyages into the unconscious, even though there are unusual juxtapositions to be found (horses chewing at bike tyres, a donkey drawn on the sand).

In his own way I think the view of England that Cliff portrays is as distinctive as those created by Hughes or Larkin:

> There used to be
> smugglers here and someone wrote 'LULU'
> four feet high in the slipway's wet concrete.

It is a vision of in-between places, where nothing much happens or promises to: where the horses snack on bike chains, boats are called Freedom, dogs run sideways, and the seaside donkeys are virtual.

Prosser

In winter two kinds of fields on the hills
outside Prosser: fields of new green wheat, the slips
rising overnight out of the plowed ground,
and waiting,
and then rising again, and budding.
Geese love this green wheat.
I ate some of it once too, to see.

And wheat stubble-fields that reach to the river.
These are the fields that have lost everything.
At night they try to recall their youth,
but their breathing is slow and irregular as
their life sinks into dark furrows.
Geese love this shattered wheat also.
They will die for it.

But everything is forgotten, nearly everything,
and sooner rather than later, please God –
fathers, friends, they pass
into your life and out again, a few women stay
a while, then go, and the fields
turn their backs, disappear in rain.
Everything goes, but Prosser.

Those nights driving back through miles of wheat fields –
headlamps raking the fields on the curves –
Prosser, that town, shining as we break over hills,
heater rattling, tired through to bone,
the smell of gunpowder on our fingers still:
I can barely see him, my father, squinting
through the windshield of that cab, saying, Prosser.

RAYMOND CARVER

All of Us: The Collected Poems (Harvill Press, 1996), by permission of The Random House Group.

■ I first read 'Prosser' in the bookshop in Northwood, where I grew up, on my way into work and back from it. This was a time in my life which I associate with beginning to put writing at the forefront of everything I thought about and did. But it was not easy. I had met one other person who wrote, a colleague. I did not belong to any writers' (or readers') groups. There was certainly no internet to play with.

In those days I travelled to London, on the Metropolitan line, to a church hall behind Euston station where the group of people I worked with would run workshops in arts-based domains for "at risk" groups in North London: old people's homes; psychiatric day-centres; reminiscence groups and so on.

I quickly learned that mornings did not always start on time at the centre. So on the way to the tube I would sneak into Northwood Books and read pages of Raymond Carver's *Fires: Essays, Poems, Stories*. In truth I gulped these pages down, devouring them in secret, replacing the book each day in a slightly different place so that no one else would find and then buy it.

Eventually I gave in, of course, and took it home. And everywhere else.

This was the first place that I had found any advice for writers ('On Writing', 'Fires', 'John Gardner: The Writer As Teacher'). It was also the first time I had the sensation of finding a voice that was talking directly to me. It is now commonplace to comment that Carver's stories, built with simple sounding language, have a clear poetic aspect: 'He could hear her ragged breathing over the sound of the air that rushed by outside. He turned off the radio and was glad for privacy' ('The Pheasant'). And I can still remember barely being able to breathe when I finished the story 'So Much Water So Close to Home' for the first time: nothing I'd read before had given me such an intensely physical reaction.

Of all the poems in *Fires* it is 'Prosser' I love the most. From the joke at the end of the first stanza to its apparent artlessness and barehanded emotion, I relish how it captures that pre-verbal monosyllabic state of utter exhaustion when driving late at night. I have always liked real names in poetry; the name of Prosser here is imbued with startling power, I think. Partly this is through repetition. Also, this happens in a figurative sense because it becomes a symbol of what is memorable, both spoken and not, between father and son.

Finally it is to do with the craft of the poem, in particular the poet's handling of sounds to create mood and atmosphere. The final stanza is dominated by 'i', 'e' ('wheat', 'fields', 'windshield'), 'l' and 't' sounds. In the first line 'nights' chimes with 'driving' which chimes with 'miles'; these are picked up in 'shining' and 'tired'. The hard 't's' of 'that', 'town', 'heater', 'rattling', 'still' and 'squinting' enact the material, the relentlessness of the journey and the need to stay awake.

Part of this music is set up with rhyming or chiming pairs of words: 'hills'/'still'; 'smell'/'barely'; 'smell'/'still'; 'gunpowder'/ 'fingers'; 'see him'/'squinting'. 'Prosser', with its eiderdown 'o', 's' and 'r' sounds works in opposition to all of these and is placed deliberately at the end of the poem, calling attention to its difference in terms of sound, but also to itself as goal or destination. It is not impossible that the 'difference' between the two men, symbolised in a small-town name, is integral to the poem's meaning.

Quoting an Isaac Babel short story in one of his essays on writing, Carver says: 'No iron can pierce the heart with such force as a period put just at the right place.' That's the way I felt about 'Prosser' when I first read it, and the way I still feel about it now: pierced. I sensed, as Seamus Heaney says of Robert Lowell, 'a whole meaning simultaneously clicking shut and breaking open, a momentous illusion that the fulfilments in the ear spelled out meanings and fulfilments available in the world.'

Wind

This house has been far out at sea all night,
The woods crashing through darkness, the booming hills,
Winds stampeding the fields under the window
Floundering black astride and blinding wet

Till day rose; then under an orange sky
The hills had new places, and wind wielded
Blade-light, luminous black and emerald,
Flexing like the lens of a mad eye.

At noon I scaled along the house-side as far as
The coal-house door. Once I looked up –
Through the brunt wind that dented the balls of my eyes
The tent of the hills drummed and strained its guyrope,

The fields quivering, the skyline a grimace,
At any second to bang and vanish with a flap:
The wind flung a magpie away and a black-
Back gull bent like an iron bar slowly. The house

Rang like some fine green goblet in the note
That any second would shatter it. Now deep
In chairs, in front of the great fire, we grip
Our hearts and cannot entertain book, thought,

Or each other. We watch the fire blazing,
And feel the roots of the house move, but sit on,
Seeing the window tremble to come in,
Hearing the stones cry out under the horizons.

TED HUGHES

Collected Poems of Ted Hughes (Faber & Faber, 2003)

■ Just about everyone I know who reads and writes poetry seriously owes a debt of one kind or another to Ted Hughes, directly or indirectly. Even though I never met him (the nearest I came was receipt of a hand-written note in the summer before he died) I still think of him as the single biggest influence on my poetry-writing (and therefore reading) life. As Peter Sansom said when Hughes died, his death was the first of a public figure that moved me personally.

These are grand claims, but they are true. It was the poetry of Ted Hughes which first alerted me to the concept of poetry which was not a hymn or a nursery rhyme. It was the poetry of Ted Hughes which I first understood as belonging to and coming from 'a poet', a living one at that, and not just a name in an anthology. And finally it was in Ted Hughes's poems which I found for the first time, aged thirteen, a sense of excitement in the act of reading.

Specifically, this was the first time I remember experiencing that vertiginous yet intimate sensation of reading poems which were not about me whilst sensing that they knew absolutely everything about me at the same time. In the English lessons we looked at 'Retired Colonel', 'Thistles', 'Pike' and (of course) 'The Thought-Fox'. Later I remember being given the poem 'Wind' to write about in an exam, and found that I could. I can still remember the weird and not altogether comforting sense of self-awareness that interpreting the poem's images gave me. I particularly enjoyed the 'black-/back gull bent like an iron bar slowly'.

In the week that Ted Hughes died I was staying at the house he had owned and lived in, Lumb Bank, now owned by the Arvon Foundation, near Heptonstall in Yorkshire. Siân Hughes and I had been asked to work alongside prizewinning young poets who were being tutored by Jo Shapcott and Roger McGough.

In the way of the old joke, it only rained twice that week, once for three days, and once for four. In the brief hiatus between these downpours, the sun did shine with what 'Wind' calls 'blade-light'. It filled the dining-room where we sat writing, the only time we saw it that week. After setting us our morning exercise, I noticed that Jo left the room. Five minutes later she silently beckoned Siân and me to follow her into the kitchen, where she whispered to us the news. At that exact moment telephones began ringing in the house, which she wisely told us to ignore.

From then on we had two main concerns: to protect the young poets from the gaze of the outside world (there were sightings of film crews near the grave of Sylvia Plath in Heptonstall); and to honour the memory of this great man whose life had touched all of ours so deeply. The first we achieved quickly. Jo broke the news to the group around the table, and we held an impromptu minute's silence. We got them to agree to a self-imposed curfew, also immaculately observed. As Seamus Heaney says in one of his sonnets of grief for his mother 'we all knew one thing by being there'.

Later that night, around the hearth of the house, Jo read 'Wind' in his honour, and we toasted his memory. The windows did indeed tremble to come in and we all felt the roots of the house move below us. Every one of us saw that the very house Hughes wrote about in the poem had now become as tangible inside our heads as the elements outside.

Jo closed by saying that her lasting memory of Ted Hughes would be one of personal encouragement, particularly in letters and in personal conversations. 'It is the side of him the world will never see,' she said, 'because kindness does not sell papers. Let that be your legacy to each other.'

'We're still here'

Magpiety

You pull over to the shoulder
of the two-lane
road and sit for a moment wondering
where you were going
in such a hurry. The valley is burned
out, the oaks
dream day and night of rain
which never comes.
At noon or just before noon
the short shadows
are gray and hold what little
life survives.
In the still heat the engine
clicks, although
the real heat is hours ahead.
You get out and step
cautiously over a low wire
fence and begin
the climb up the yellowed hill.
A hundred feet
ahead the trunks of two
fallen oaks
rust; something passes over
them, a lizard
perhaps or a trick of sight.
The next tree
you pass is unfamiliar,
the trunk dark,
as black as an olive's; the low
branches stab
out, gnarled and dull: a carob
or a Joshua tree.
A sudden flaring-up ahead,

a black-winged
bird rises from nowhere,
white patches
underneath its wings, and is gone.
You hear your own
breath catching in your ears,
a roaring, a sea
sound that goes on and on
until you lean
forward to place both hands
– fingers spread –
into the bleached grasses
and let your knees
slowly down. Your breath slows
and you know
you're back in central
California
on your way to San Francisco
or the coastal towns
with their damp sea breezes
you haven't
even a hint of. But first
you must cross
the Pacheco Pass. People
expect you, and yet
you remain, still leaning forward
into the grasses
that if you could hear them
would tell you
all you need to know about
the life ahead.

Out of a sense of modesty
or to avoid the truth
I've been writing in the second
person, but in truth

it was I, not you, who pulled
        the green Ford
over to the side of the road
        and decided to get
up that last hill to look
        back at the valley
he'd come to call home.
        I can't believe
that man, only thirty-two,
        less than half
my age, could be the person
        fashioning these lines.
That was late July of '60.
        I had heard
all about magpies, how they
        snooped and meddled
in the affairs of others, not
        birds so much
as people. If you dared
        to remove a wedding
ring as you washed away
        the stickiness of love
or the cherished odors of another
        man or woman,
as you turned away
        from the mirror
having admired your new-found
        potency – humming
'My Funny Valentine' or
        'Body and Soul' –
to reach for a rough towel
        or some garment
on which to dry yourself,
        he would enter
the open window behind you
        that gave gratefully

onto the fields and the roads
        bathed in dawn –
he, the magpie – and snatch
        up the ring
in his hard beak and shoulder
        his way back
into the currents of the world
        on his way
to the only person who could
        change your life:
a king or a bride or an old woman
        asleep on her porch.

Can you believe the bird
        stood beside you
just long enough, though far
        smaller than you
but fearless in a way
        a man or woman
could never be? An apparition
        with two dark
and urgent eyes and motions
        so quick and precise
they were barely motions at all?
        When he was gone
you turned, alarmed by the rustling
        of oily feathers
and the curious pungency,
        and were sure
you'd heard him say the words
        that could explain
the meaning of blond grasses
        burning on a hillside
beneath the hands of a man
        in the middle of
his life caught in the posture

of prayer. I'd
heard that a magpie could talk,
so I waited
for the words, knowing without
the least doubt
what he'd do, for up ahead
an old woman
waited on her wide front porch.
My children
behind her house played
in a silted pond
poking sticks at the slow
carp that flashed
in the fallen sunlight. You
are thirty-two
only once in your life, and though
July comes
too quickly, you pray for
the overbearing
heat to pass. It does, and
the year turns
before it holds still for
even a moment.
Beyond the last carob
or Joshua tree
the magpie flashes his sudden
wings; a second
flames and vanishes into the pale
blue air.
July 23, 1960.
I lean down
closer to hear the burned grasses
whisper all I
need to know. The words rise
around me, separate
and finite. A yellow dust

rises and stops
caught in the noon's driving light.
Three ants pass
across the back of my reddened
right hand.
Everything is speaking or singing.
We're still here.

PHILIP LEVINE

Stranger to Nothing: Selected Poems (Bloodaxe Books, 2006)

■ In September 2006 my treatment for non-Hodgkin's lymphoma came to an end. I was not told I was officially in remission from the disease for another month.

It was a very difficult time. On one level I missed the routine of being treated for cancer. Even the radiology centre, with its slab and windowless rooms, had provided each day with some sort of purpose. Now, with my children's return to school, and my wife's to work after the holiday break, there was just me…

Reading books, unthinkable during chemotherapy treatment, began to seem appealing again. Ditto the newspaper. Even the odd glass of wine.

Except that they weren't. Experience quickly taught me – my eyes glazing over, hangover-like headaches after the first sip – that re-entry into "normal" life was going to be anything but easy. Plus I was still overweight. I would wheeze, even on a trip to buy milk.

My visitors dried up.

I found the slightest thing would make me cry: an overheard song on the radio; my children's laughter; meeting my colleagues again.

It was in this listless atmosphere that I discovered Philip Levine's 'Magpiety'. Levine's poetry had been recommended to me some years before, and I had responded by buying three of his books, devouring them greedily in quick succession. *Stranger to Nothing* was different, though, a British selection of his work, a first. Even though I did not have the money, I persuaded myself I needed it.

The house once again empty, I shuffled into town one Saturday afternoon and spent a happy half-hour in Waterstones sampling its pages.

'Magpiety' is the poem the book opened to on the bus home. Though it corresponds to no event or landscape in my life that I can remember, I distinctly remember coming up against the sensation of having encountered it before. Laced into its tough and dreamy narrative was an elemental vocabulary I knew Levine returned to over and again in his poems: 'truth', 'rain', 'night', 'survives', 'heat', 'breath', 'love', 'knees', 'words', 'dust', 'woman' and 'man'.

It was like that scene in *Stand by Me*, when the boys bend to put their ears to the railway tracks they are walking along to discern the advent of a coming train with a shrug and a bravado 'Nah!' The bus and its passengers seemed to have started listing in the afternoon sunshine. Fluids streamed from my eyes, nose and mouth. Knowing I was in trouble but pretending I was not, I read the extraordinary affirmation of life in the poem's final lines, word by word, repeatedly, until my breathing calmed.

Stepping off the bus in the same town, and yet an entirely different one, I allowed myself to take it as a sign, not that I was out of the woods, nor even that I had a path through them, but that I no longer faced it alone.

Tamoxifen

My doctor's given me a massive can
of elephant repellent. I'm to spray

it, after washing, on my skin. It will
substantially reduce the risk, he says

of being trampled by an elephant
in Saville Row, The Side or Grainger Street.

I'm terrified of elephants, of course
but never have I seen one roam the streets

of Tyneside. That's the point, my doctor says
as if their absence proves the potency

of elephant repellent. Problem is,
the spray's a vivid blue and permanent

so I'd be branded like some miscreant –
my only crime, susceptibility

to elephant advances. Worst of all
I won't be able to forget my plight.

And how can I be sure the spray will work?
And how long must I use the wretched stuff?

Five years…that long? What choices do I have?
I spray, and hope, and bear the mark, or risk

the onslaught of an errant elephant
one unsuspecting day. Well, thank you, doc

but no, I won't be cowed: my life's too short
to waste in fear. Five years is far too long,

the benefit does not outweigh the risk.
Instead I'll stride out blithely every day

and if by chance I meet an elephant
perhaps I'll have some peanuts in my bag

and as it's said that they cannot resist
the taste of nuts, well, maybe I'll survive.

ALISON MOSQUERA

The Poetry Cure, ed. Julia Darling and Cynthia Fuller (Bloodaxe Books, 2005), by permission of the author.

■ My interest in 'Tamoxifen' rests largely on my experience of teaching it in a series of workshops about poetry and health. It was an attempt to connect my lifelong interest in poetry and my more recently acquired obsession with the language of cancer in our culture, specifically the clichés of 'battles' and 'fighting' the disease.

Towards the end of the course I thought it was important to look at some poems that tackled this issue by offering alternatives to this martial discourse. One of these was Alison Mosquera's 'Tamoxifen'.

Uniquely in my experience of workshopping poems, it provoked an immediate cry of 'Oh God!' while I was still handing copies of the poem round the group. It is one of the unwritten rules of workshops that I conduct that no one is required at any point to discuss their personal lives or history: we discuss the poetry, not the biography.

Nevertheless, I was intrigued.

The force and unmediated nature of this comment reminded me of a comment I once heard a preacher make about another, very different 'Oh God' moment in literature. The speaker chose as his text chapter 17 of John's Gospel, with a concentrated focus on verse 1. The Last Supper now complete, Jesus starts to pray, beginning with the words 'Oh God…'.

Normally, he said, we skate over this to get to the content, but he went at great lengths to say how this guttural utterance was the main content of the prayer. The extraordinary tone of this moment, largely missing in translation, is one of grief and exhaustion. It was, he said, the poem we all pray *in extremis*: when we are lonely or diagnosed; when we come home to an empty house; when we have been abused or denied justice, whether we believe in God or not. He called it the ur-prayer of all humanity, recognised across religions and races and ethnicities. He said it was as near to pre-verbal utterance as prayer or poetry could get, a whole universe of suffering summed up in two syllables.

This is what I thought of as we discussed 'Tamoxifen' that evening. We had many brilliant things to say about it, not least its deadpan humour, controlled handling of natural speech, plus that amazing metaphor of the elephant. But in a way the main job of critiquing the poem, and speaking honestly about it, had already been done.

The bookbinder

Pare the leather, thin the skin
where it must stretch and crease.
Then paste: the tanned flesh darkens,

wet and chill, fingers working
over spine and cords, into joints,
mitreing corners neat and flat.

Bandage the book in paper, let it
settle under weights, day after day
until the leather's dry and tight.

When the time is right for finishing,
black the room, clamp the book
spine up in the beechwood press,

the lamp pointing where to begin.
Hot brass letters and a vigilant hand –
an accurate blind impression.

Paint in glair with a fine brush,
lay on gold leaf, with level breath.
Tilt the light, shadows will reveal

the place to press the tool again.
Now, strike the gold – feel the title
word by word, bright in the grain.

CLARE BEST
Excisions (Waterloo Press, 2011)

■ I first came across Clare Best's poetry at a reading. She was taking part in an event which brought together Clare, a photographer, a medical practitioner, a psychologist, a cultural historian and a literary critic to explore the issue of preventative medicine, cancer and our perceptions about the body.

To listen to Clare speak about her preventive double mastectomy, with accompanying poems, was a revelation. It is commonplace for artists to use their biographies as material for their work, but less so to encounter such a rich and strange transformation in their presentation of the actuality. In the words of her publisher, this is indeed 'pioneer territory', which explores 'how it feels to experience radical surgery and its aftermath in a society permeated by orthodox ideas of perfection and beauty'.

Poem after poem in 'Self-portrait without breasts', the central section of *Excisions*, takes the reader unsparingly through the process of diagnosis, surgery, recuperation and aftermath. The best of these turn on fictions and images not always allied to the narrative in hand, telling it altogether more powerfully for telling it slant.

My favourite of these is 'The bookbinder'. The conceit of the poem, apparent from the first line ('Pare the leather, thin the skin / where it must stretch and crease'), links the bookbinder's trade to that of a surgeon. Everything in the poem is solid, yet freighted with extra meaning, coming at it does right at the end of the 'self-portrait' sequence. It is a poem of flesh, 'fingers working / over spine and cords, into joints.'

Written in short sentences based on terse, imperative verbs, the poem describes the bookbinder laying on gold leaf 'with level breath'. That phrase could serve as a description of the book's procedures as a whole, which is remarkably even in tone. To call work of this kind 'brave' is trite (and, personally speaking, the last thing a patient/sufferer usually wants to hear). Nevertheless, we need to recognise innovative and ground-breaking work when we see it, whether that is achieved in tone, content or form. Clare Best masters all three in *Excisions*. We need more books like it.

from In the Wake of Home

But you will be drawn to places
where generations lie
side by side with each other:
fathers, mothers and children
in the family prayerbook
or the country burying-ground
You will hack your way back through the bush
to the Jodensavanne
where the gravestones are black with mould
You will stare at old family albums
with their smiles   their resemblances
You will want to believe that nobody
wandered off   became strange
no woman dropped her baby and ran
no father took off for the hills
no axe splintered the door
– that once at least it was all in order
and nobody came to grief

ADRIENNE RICH

Your Native Land, Your Life (W.W. Norton, 1986), by permission of W.W. Norton & Company, Inc.

■ In 1991 I made the decision to teach part-time so that I could put poetry more at the centre of my life. I was still new to the game of submitting my work to magazines, but had learned enough to get by, quickly making virtual friends with far-off names like *Scratch*, *Fatchance*, *The North* and *Smiths Knoll*.

It was a heady time. The drop in my income was now challenged by a weekly list of new temptations: Bloodaxe catalogues, *The Poet's Manual and Rhyming Dictionary*, subscribing to *Poetry Review*. Just as important was a slim red book recommended to me by someone at a workshop, Julia Casterton's *Creative Writing: A Practical Guide* (Macmillan). It was like nothing I had ever read, down to earth: honest and passionate. Its pages burst with quotes and one liners by writers about writing and other writers. It was a bit like being invited to a party at a very eclectic and learned Senior Common Room, where all the dons assumed you were as well-read as they were.

One of the book's presiding and central spirits is Adrienne Rich. The quotations from her work which Casterton chose were simultaneously dense and shockingly clear, alive with anger at history and silence:

> The present breaks our hearts. We lie and freeze,
> our fingers icy as a bunch of keys.
> Nothing will thaw these bones except
> memory like and ancient blanket wrapped
> about us when we sleep at home again,
> smelling of picnics, closets, sicknesses,
> old nightmare,
> and insomnia's spreading stain.
> ('Readings of History')

This chimed with Casterton's own worldview, prefigured in sub-headings which had titles such as 'Conversing with the spirits of place', 'Writing your own conflict' and 'Writing with the whole self'.

She used Rich's extraordinary long poem 'In the Wake of Home' to demonstrate Fowler's preferences for writing in *The King's English*:

1. Prefer the familiar word to the far-fetched
2. Prefer the concrete word to the abstract.
3. Prefer the single word to the circumlocution.
4. Prefer the Saxon word to the Romance.
5. Prefer the short word to the long.

Casterton said: now look how Rich does it.

It felt to me on first reading as though the speaker had somehow intuited knowledge and information about the deepest and unspoken parts of my family history and stripped them bare for all to see. On subsequent readings the voice lost none of this force, gathering in strength and humanity for being so close, so plain and within earshot. It was like encountering a sardonic aunt who takes you to one side at a family gathering to whisper: you kids, don't believe everything you've been told. 'Look at these adjectives', Casterton says: 'family, country, black, old, strange... Note particularly the total absence of adverbs.'

This was not deconstructing a poem as we had done at school. This was saying: there is moral and political and ethical force in the choices of words you make to say what you have to say, so you better use and choose the right ones.

This was writing as committed and serious work. Reading the poem confronted all my preconceived ideas about 'writing what I knew'. This challenge pulsed in every line. The good news was I now had a yardstick to measure my own attempts at growth.

To My Heart at the Close of Day

At dusk light you come to bat
As Georg Trakl might put it. How are you doing
Aside from that, aside from the fact
That you are at bat? What balls are you going to hit
Into the outfield, what runs will you score,
And do you think you ever will, eventually,
Bat one out of the park? That would be a thrill
To you and your contemporaries! Your mighty posture
Takes its stand in my chest and swing swing swing
You warm up, then you take a great step
Forward as the ball comes smashing toward you, home
Plate. And suddenly it is evening.

KENNETH KOCH

■ I first came across this poem in the review of *New Addresses*, from which it comes, by Mark Halliday in *Poetry Review*. If you will forgive the pun, I felt it was the game-changer. There is something more than autumnal about the piece, the voice dropping to a conversational murmur which is intimate and troubled. In a poem about a summer pastime which is played out on a grand scale in front of crowds, this is refreshingly ironic.

I think the poem is playful on other levels (please forgive that pun also). I think Koch is playing with his public persona of wackiness. Read the first four and a half lines out loud: there is more than a hint of Edward Lear about them. I think his contemporaries also ghost this poem, with the inevitable comparisons that were and are and probably always will be made between that famous school of New Yorkers, who were after all friends who supported and encouraged each other.

I delight in this poem, even though I know next to nothing about baseball.

Underneath all of these plays for attention, the poem unleashes the twin terrors of a ball coming 'smashing toward you' in the 'sudden' darkness. The 'great step' we take toward it may indeed be a 'thrill', but the poem is careful not to prescribe anything so definite as an outcome.

Finally I think Koch is playing with the idea of poems being words that can knock you for six (forgive the pun). That is what this one does to me.

Photograph in a Stockholm Newspaper for March 13, 1910

Here is a family so little famous
their names were not recorded. They stand,
indistinct as though they know it's right,
in this slum courtyard
in weak sunlight. The darksuited father's hand
rests on his small son's shoulder,
mother and daughter are on either side
of the open door. It is a Sunday
or we may suppose they would not be
together like this, motionless
for the photographer's early art.

To be moved by these people must seem sentimental.
We're here years too late
to hope their blurred faces will unpack
into features we can side with
or against, or expect these bodies
will continue into those next shapes
on which we'll base a plot.

But that's it: not *here they are*, but
there they were. Safe now from even
their own complexities – what luck
not to be asked their names! – and proof
against our most intricate pursuit,
they stand in a blur that seems
no error of focus but an inspired rendering
of how they chose to last,
admitting nothing except that once
they were. That hand rested
on that shoulder. The four of them stood there.
There was a little sunlight.

We shall never learn more. They seem
miraculous. They persuade me
all will be well.

DON COLES

Someone Has Stayed in Stockholm: New and Selected Poems (Arc, 1994)

■ I have one book of Don Coles, the UK publication by the heroic Arc Publications of his *Someone Has Stayed in Stockholm.* If you do not know it, it is a completely transformative book, taking the reader into new and uncharted imaginative territories, and I urge you to buy it.

There are poems here in the voice of Kafka in love, taken from his letters and journals; a long sequence of poems about Edvard Munch 'and his (largely untranslated diaries)'; found poetry using the *Michelin Guide*; and some startling meditations on mortality and ageing, particularly the sequence of poems 'Landslides (Visits to the Gericare Centre)'. As some of these titles and themes suggest, the book feels very European, not North American, in its sensibility.

(I only ever read one UK review of it, by Martin Stannard, and would be grateful to see more…)

I seem to remember Stannard saying about 'Photograph in a Stockholm Newspaper for March 13, 1910' something along the lines that it takes a corny, old hat idea, 'writing from a postcard', and transforms it into something altogether more rich and strange than the material has any right to offer.

The poem achieves this by containing very little actual description or reporting on the visual material; it is much more of a meditation, in a recursive and speculative way, about how humans choose 'to last'. The poem is aware of 'complexities' of each individual in the photograph, but does not attempt to extricate these or spell them out. In making the reader aware of this awareness the poem seems to enter into a zone of calm yet tense reflexivity which gives us only minor hints of what is going on: 'they stand in a blur'; 'the darksuited father's hand/ rests on his small son's shoulder'; there is 'weak sunlight'.

These details are sketchy, deliberately it seems to me, but they are enough, because the miraculous closing lines, which ask us to credit evidence of the miraculous in meagre circumstances, come across not as assertion, but rather a blossoming of the idea of the possibility of 'lasting' at all.

Let Evening Come

Let the light of late afternoon
shine through chinks in the barn, moving
up the bales as the sun moves down.

Let the cricket take up chafing
as a woman takes up her needles
and her yarn. Let evening come.

Let dew collect on the hoe abandoned
in long grass. Let the stars appear
and the moon disclose her silver horn.

Let the fox go back to its sandy den.
Let the wind die down. Let the shed
go black inside. Let evening come.

To the bottle in the ditch, to the scoop
in the oats, to air in the lung
let evening come.

Let it come, as it will, and don't
be afraid. God does not leave us
comfortless, so let evening come.

JANE KENYON

■ A couple of weeks after I finished my radiotherapy treatment for non-Hodgkin's lymphoma in October 2006 I bought Jane Kenyon's *Let Evening Come*. This in itself felt like some kind of victory. One of the lesser-known effects of chemotherapy treatment for cancer is its comprehensive annihilation of the patient's ability to concentrate. On anything. Susan Sontag famously compared it to having a stroke. She called it 'chemobrain'.

By this stage of my treatment (I hesitate to say 'journey' and am reluctant to say 'battle') I pretty much knew that I would survive the disease. Nevertheless I spent much of each day moping around the house unable to settle to anything and welling up with tears at the slightest thing: music on car adverts; babies; visitors (or the lack of them).

The thick skin I had spent all of my adult life cultivating was suddenly stripped bare. My counsellor called it Post Traumatic Stress Disorder.

Naturally in my British way I thought this was poppycock and nearly walked out. The fact is I knew she was right. And besides, I did not exactly have much choice in the matter. Though it was rather exposing, I remember taking courage from Stephen Fry's documentary *The Secret Life of the Manic Depressive*. In such random ways do we feel ever so slightly less alone.

My other touchstone at this time was *Let Evening Come*. I am not even sure how I came to want to buy it (I think it was a review). It is a lovely, lovely book and you should own a copy. As someone once said about Robert Nye's poetry, it is the sort of book you should read with a loved one and a bottle of wine on top of a hill watching the sunset.

It is no secret that Jane Kenyon suffered with bipolar disorder. She died from a virulent form of leukaemia in April 1995. For these and many more details about her life you should turn to the book's excellent and honest Introduction and essay-memoir by her friend Joyce Peseroff and husband Donald Hall respectively.

What comes across in both these and the poems is Kenyon's absolute dedication to her craft, to her family and to the natural world. In everything she wrote she seemed to maintain the same clear-eyed focus and levelness of tone, in subjects as different as a vase of chrysanthemums, preparing the evening meal or her new drug combinations. Far from diluting the poems' power this gives them extra force and stillness: the horror, when it arrives, comes not in a screech but a whisper.

The title-poem 'Let Evening Come' came into my life, therefore, at a time when I was tired, more than a little on edge and predisposed to looking for confirmation that life might continue to go on, and that, if and when it did, it might contain good things. 'Let Evening Come' confirms and affirms the expectation of life in every single one of its lines. I read it now in different circumstances of course, but remain in debt to its plain-speaking evocation of 'light of late afternoon', albeit visible in 'chinks'.

The Middle Kingdom

In those days we spent our time
sitting quietly in softly lighted rooms
designed for that purpose, trying not
to let any involuntary line of thought
arrive at its logical (and, of course,
regrettable) conclusion: namely
that our days were numbered.

We were all well-fed and warmly clothed,
and experienced no misgivings on this account.
The oceans were calm and shallow,
the rivers stocked with salmon. Each spring
brilliantly coloured birds passed over
on their way to northern lakes and hills.
Poems were often penned concerning
their brief and glorious transit. When
they returned in autumn we succumbed
to appropriate feelings of mild regret.

Our figurative art gave no hint of the fact
that male animals experienced erections,
nor were children obliged to light the match
that would incinerate their families.
Similarly It was not considered necessary
to rip your opponent's lips from his face,
or force him to digest his ears.

How slow that time now seems,
how sweet, how gradual every graceful gesture!
But it is impossible to regret its passing.
It was not a time of truth and realism.
The passage of migratory birds
did not accord to the facts, nor

the coming of spring, nor the love of mothers
for their children, nor a man's respect
for women, nor courtesy, friendship, honour...

Regret is impossible
(and, besides, nostalgia
is an imprisonable offense) now
that every issue is as clear as blood,
bright as tears, and we live
in understanding even as we die.

JOHN ASH

The Burnt Pages (Carcanet Press, 1991)

■ One of the pleasures of being alive is reading John Ash.

Think of a prize-winning poet, someone you think of as a poetry household-name: that's how good John Ash is and how well-known he should be. I have a strong suspicion that none of this means a jot to him, which makes me enjoy his work even more.

I first came across his work in Cliff Yates's great book of teaching poetry, *Jumpstart*; which contains a marvellous poem of faux-instructions of Ash: 'Some Words of Advice: After Hesiod'. The poem opens:

> Never believe the words you hear in popular songs.
> Conversely, believe them all,
> even the ones about changing the world and living forever.

This is a microcosm of many of Ash's procedures: the importance (or complete irrelevance) of words; a relish in artefacts of popular culture; and a profound sense of decay. Most of all, these lines have a conversational lightness of tone, a characteristic he shares with the late Kenneth Koch who used to say that just because his poems were not solemn did not mean they were not to be taken seriously.

'Some Words of Advice' led me to buy Ash's *Selected Poems* which of course it did not contain. By this time I had read Ash's poem 'Smoke' in Peter Sansom's terrific *Writing Poems*. This poem also contains references to 'snatches of show tunes in the corridors' and 'old arias of desire', but now the tone is chastened, cautious, elegiac:

> In a city of burnt throats there can never be
> enough sweet water to start the songs
> and if you would dance, you must dance to the memory
> of that lighted window the dusk carried off

Both 'Smoke' and 'Some Words of Advice' are contained in the second book of Ash's poems based in New York, *The Burnt Pages*, where he moved in 1985.

If you do not know it, it is a seriously important piece of work. Without wishing to be reductive, it is as critical to our understanding of AIDS as the perhaps more famous *The Man with Night Sweats* (Thom Gunn), *My Alexandria* (Mark Doty) and *What the Living Do* (Marie Howe):

> What is left is irretrievable,
> but continues like a melody
> whose logical and grieving progression nothing can halt.
>
> ('In Rainy Country')

The book is about much more than that, of course, but I do think, in poems like 'The Middle Kingdom', 'Smoke', 'Cigarettes', 'My Egypt', 'Following a Man', 'The Sweeping Gesture', 'Forgetting' and 'In Rainy Country' Ash performs a sustained mediation on mortality and decay that is both exquisite and what Peter Sansom calls 'urgent'.

For my money 'The Middle Kingdom' fuses together two of *The Burnt Pages*' chief impulses: clear-eyed satire and deep personal 'regret', a word the poem uses three times:

> We were all well-fed and warmly clothed,
> and experienced no misgivings on this account.
> The oceans were calm and shallow,
> the rivers stocked with salmon. Each spring
> brilliantly coloured birds passed over
> on their way to northern lakes and hills.
> Poems were often penned concerning
> their brief and glorious transit. When
> they returned in autumn we succumbed
> to appropriate feelings of mild regret.

You should read this, and everything by John Ash. His work, including his recent work about living in Istanbul, never fails to take the reader into wholly new territories both real and imagined, living and historical. His poems never let you forget the forces of history in which they were created, and which they notate, but neither do they bash down your door as they remind you of this. I think he is one of the greats.

The Journey

One day you finally knew
what you had to do, and began,
though the voices around you
kept shouting
their bad advice –
though the whole house
began to tremble
and you felt the old tug
at your ankles.
'Mend my life!'
each voice cried.
But you didn't stop.
You knew what you had to do,
though the wind pried
with its stiff fingers
at the very foundations,
though their melancholy
was terrible.
It was already late
enough, and a wild night,
and the road full of fallen
branches and stones.
But little by little,
as you left their voices behind,
the stars began to burn
through the sheets of clouds,
and there was a new voice
which you slowly
recognised as your own,
that kept you company
as you strode deeper and deeper
into the world,
determined to do

the only thing you could do –
determined to save
the only life you could save.

MARY OLIVER

■ As I was with the work of Billy Collins I am pretty much the last person to come to the Mary Oliver party. It took an evening of noodling around on the internet searching for something else for me to discover her properly. I had felt Oliver's searching and tough-delicate poems kind of bouncing off me a little. I am not proud of it; but it is true.

It came in the form of a blog post by my friend Malcolm Doney, in which he retold the story of Jeremy Paxman grilling Russell Brand on *Newsnight*, in the wake of the fallout from his prank call, with Jonathan Ross, to Andrew Sachs. I never saw the programme in question but feel as though I have. Brand stated that there are two Russell Brands, the one people go to see and hear, expecting something miraculous, and the idiot who makes prank phone calls. He confessed to making the same mistake himself, thinking he was phoning up Manuel from *Fawlty Towers*, not somebody's grandfather. He believed in the icon, not the man.

Not least among the pleasures of reading Malcolm's piece, therefore, was the physical sensation of feeling my preconceived ideas about Brand being turned on their head. From the sound of it, this is what Jeremy Paxman went through as well.

Paxman concluded the programme with this reflection, that there was important terrain for us to explore between 'external validation and internal validation': 'a matter in essence, of finding yourself, beyond other people's expectations' as Malcolm so eloquently put it. At that point Malcolm's piece stops; he lets Mary Oliver do the talking instead. Her poem is a life lesson I can never learn too often.

mercifully ordain that we may become aged together

Tobit 8.7

I was in the Canadian Muffin Company in Armada Way,
waiting for an extra large latte, cinnamon and chocolate
and a white chocolate chip muffin, to take away,
when I saw them. He was helping her get into her coat.
He held it out for her as if the sleeves were winged
while she gracefully turned her back to shrug it on.
At this point he did a little jink, more of an imperceptible
hoick, on the balls of his feet, so the coat lifted
neatly over her shoulders and tucked under her neck,
then he freed her hair from the collar. He must have
done this for years, this exact same thing for years.
I watched him pick up the shopping, she picked up
her bag, and I collected my latte and my white
chocolate chip muffin and walked out into the rain.

ANN GRAY

At the Gate (Headland Books, 2008), by permission of the author

■ I first came across 'mercifully ordain that we may become aged together' in *The Rialto*. It is taken from Ann's collection *At the Gate*, and shares what I think of as that book's central preoccupation: how can we live with attention to those we love the most.

The poem is spoken in an easy-going demotic which belies its cleverness. It flirts with becoming a well-behaved sonnet, then veers off at the fifth line, as if it has more important business in mind.

All that happens is a man helping his wife into her coat in a coffee shop. There is no extra commentary. There is nothing complicated about the diction or the scene it describes. Yet I find it completely harrowing.

The more I read the poem the more convinced I am that the poem achieves its power in the gap between the unfulfilled promise of its title and the expression of everyday love which is described. The key to this is the 'c'/'ck' sounds in the middle of the poem, contained in the words 'jink', 'hoick', 'neck' and 'tucked'. These are like breath catching in the throat, as at the start of tears. Everything either side of them is smooth, in phrasing which chimes in pairs of words: 'shoulders'/'shopping', 'feet'/'freed', 'helping'/ 'held'. This is re-emphasised in the repeated 'He must have / done this for years, this exact same thing for years.'

The entrance and exit of the poem's speaker are also paired in the details they contain (the latte and the white chocolate chip muffin). But the speaker leaves the poem (and the Canadian Muffin Company) as she enters it, alone.

Poetry

Poetry has nothing to do with who we are.
It cannot be explained by biography,
e.g. sickness, unhappiness.
Poetry is a swart planet
with which we are in touch, from which
we receive at certain times messages.
Nor is it a black or emerald clock –
I think it is a voice which speaks to us
at night, as unquiet trembling, or maybe
a curious arrangement of stones,
poorly random and yet sonorous,
a packet of crisps beside a Greek vase
on a day with the breeze flowing from the south.

IAIN CRICHTON SMITH
New Collected Poems (Carcanet Press, 2011)

■ It was summer. I found myself on the top floor of the library, on the recommendation of a friend: 'It's where they keep the poetry.'

She did not mention it was tucked away in the furthest recess possible.

Many of the names there were predictable: Hughesheaneylarkin plath. But there were surprises too. A very complete collection of Redgrove. Poets from Ireland. Poets in translation.

You could follow the sensibility of the person who had chosen the books. For about twelve years they must have had the best fun imaginable.

It was eclectic, whimsical, untutored. Then it stops, just as the Bloodaxe explosion is about to fill the skies, the New and Next Generations a very tiny dot on an unimagined horizon.

I imagine the committee meeting which approved the cutbacks, a day like today, hot, slightly end of termish, people faithfully showing up and committing to the task in hand.

(I don't believe in agendas or conspiracy theories. I believe people follow their lights, talking and pausing and wondering and influenced by other people, for good or ill.)

Or perhaps there were no cutbacks. Perhaps the person left. Or fell ill.

The poetry stops.

Except it doesn't stop.

You can still climb those stairs to that recess and you can still find gems like this. It's an unremarkable looking book called *Ends and Beginnings*. You can still turn the pages.

There it is, on page 1, set apart from the rest of the collection, a kind of statement, wrapped up in a surprising lyric poem of thirteen lines that is like opening a window with a view onto the sea.

It is poetry and it is in your hands. The committee did not win.

Everything Is Going To Be All Right

How should I not be glad to contemplate
the clouds clearing beyond the dormer window
and a high tide reflected on the ceiling?
There will be dying, there will be dying,
but there is no need to go into that.
The lines flow from the hand unbidden
and the hidden source is the watchful heart.
The sun rises in spite of everything
and the far cities are beautiful and bright.
I lie here in a riot of sunlight
watching the day break and the clouds flying.
Everything is going to be all right.

DEREK MAHON

Collected Poems (Gallery Press, 2011) by permission of the author and The Gallery Press, Loughcrew, Oldcastle, Co. Meath, Ireland.

■ I first read Derek Mahon's 'Everything Is Going To Be All Right' as an undergraduate, somewhere towards the end of my degree, at a stage of life when everything did indeed seem hopeful and untainted by disaster and breakdown. My reaction on reading it was a kind of falling in love, infatuation followed by obsession, taking the book in which I found it (a library copy of his *Selected Poems*) everywhere and checking every ten minutes to see if it was still there.

I loved it so much I stole the title and final line in my poem 'Here', the final poem in my first book of poems *How Far From Here is Home*? I owe my discovery of many of the poets who influenced my early publishing and subsequent first book to my friend the furniture maker and designer Duncan Kramer. I can't help wondering how different my life would have been not to have known him and not to have seen *The Penguin Book of Contemporary British Poetry* sticking out of his pocket one night at a Durutti Column concert.

As Raymond Carver says in his essay 'Fires', I am talking about real *influence* here, decisions you make as a young person when you do not really know what you are doing but feel kind of right, like forming a band or deciding to move away from home, the consequences of which you cannot know at the time but which later seem to contain the essence of the matter of life and death.

Now of course I am returning to the poem as a middle-aged man and I read it completely differently. I have had cancer. The day I was told I was well again a young poet friend of mine took her own life.

The poem insists 'There will be dying, there will be dying' but immediately skirts round the issue. I like this kind of bravado in a poem, albeit in a tone of low-key assertion. I know it is not true but nevertheless while I am in what John Gardner calls the dream of its narrative I am once again prepared to believe it and live it a little stronger perhaps as I pad down the stairs to make coffee.

INDEX

Index of poets

Index of titles

Anthony Wilson is a poet, writing tutor and Senior Lecturer at the University of Exeter.

His anthology *Lifesaving Poems* – based on his popular blog – is published by Bloodaxe in 2015. His own books of poetry are *Riddance* (Worple Press, 2012), *Full Stretch: Poems 1996-2006* (Worple Press, 2006), *Nowhere Better Than This* (Worple Press, 2002) and *How Far From Here is Home?* (Stride, 1996). His memoir of cancer, *Love for Now* (Impress Books), was published in 2012.

Anthony has held writing residencies at The Poetry Society, *The Times Educational Supplement*, Apples and Snakes, Tate Britain, and The Poetry Trust, for whom he was the 2014 Aldeburgh Poetry Festival Blogger.

Anthony blogs at www.anthonywilsonpoetry.com

FSC
www.fsc.org